THE OTHER SIDE OF THE MOUNTAIN

Ian W. Shaw is an acclaimed writer of narrative nonfiction who has made an important contribution to Australian history and to Australia's understanding of itself as a nation. After a decade of school teaching and twenty-five years working as a security risk analyst for both government agencies and large private companies, Ian became a full-time writer in 2012. Ian has published seven works of Australian and military history, all of which are characterised by his ability to locate and access hidden tales from our past, and for his meticulous and far-reaching research.

BOOKS BY IAN W. SHAW

Operation Babylift

Murder at Dusk

The Rag Tag Fleet

Glenrowan

The Ghosts of Roebuck Bay

On Radji Beach

The Bloodbath

THE OTHER SIDE OF THE MOUNTAIN

How a tycoon, a pastoralist and a convict helped
shape the exploration of colonial Australia

IAN W. SHAW

Woodslane Press Pty Ltd
10 Apollo Street
Warriewood, NSW 2102
Email: info@woodslane.com.au
02 8445 2300 www.woodslane.com.au

First published in Australia in 2020 by Woodslane Press
© 2020 Woodslane Press, text © 2020 Ian W. Shaw

The information in this publication is based upon the current state of commercial and
industry practice and the general circumstances as at the date of publication. Every effort
has been made to obtain permissions relating to information reproduced in this publication.
The publisher makes no representations as to the accuracy, reliability or completeness of
the information contained in this publication. To the extent permitted by law, the publisher
excludes all conditions, warranties and other obligations in relation to the supply of this
publication and otherwise limits its liability to the recommended retail price. In no circumstances will the publisher be liable to any third party for any consequential loss or damage
suffered by any person resulting in any way from the use or reliance on this publication or
any part of it. Any opinions and advice contained in the publication are offered solely in
pursuance of the author's and publisher's intention to provide information, and have not
been specifically sought.

 A catalogue record for this
book is available from the
National Library of Australia

Printed in Australia by McPhersons
Cover images: Paintings from the Horrocks expedition, Gill, S. T. (Samuel Thomas), NLA
nla.obj-134354182-1, nla.obj-134370990-1, nla.obj-134371955-1, nla.obj-134372439-1
Book design by: Luke Harris

CONTENTS

INTRODUCTION

Bushrangers, explorers and adventurers ... *The Other Side of the Mountain* chronicles three true, but almost forgotten, stories of life, death and adventure on the colonial Australian frontier.

Although Ralph Entwistle, John Horrocks and Horace Wills are not as well-known as their more famous contemporaries, the impact that these early bushrangers, explorers and adventurers made on the development of different parts of our early Australian society should not be underestimated.

The Ribbon Boys of Bathurst recounts how a gang of bushrangers arose during the early colonisation of the well-watered grasslands and well-forested hills that lay to the west of the Blue Mountains. This area was a new frontier of challenges and possibilities for the pastoralists, small farmers and ticket of leave men, as well as the convicts who would be required to clear the land.

One convict called Ralph Entwistle was the founder and leader of the notorious Ribbon Boys; some of the earliest bushrangers in Australia. Like so many of the convicts who were transported to Australia, it was actually a relatively small mistake that triggered their uprising and lead to terrible consequences that far outweighed the original misdemeanour.

Set almost 700 miles to the south-west of Bathurst, in the new colony of South Australia, *The Great Beyond* is an example of early exploration by the English "gentlemen" who came to Australia of their own free will.

1

John Horrocks was one such gentleman, an intrepid and passionate explorer who had the wealth, the drive and the urge to commit to significant expeditions. Horrocks' journey into the semi-desert country that Bourke and Wills would more famously traverse 14 years later, was shorter than he hoped and ultimately ill fated. However, he too deserves a much more prominent place in our history books.

Horrocks had the foresight to see the benefits of using camels in exploring Australia and he went on to use the very first camel to arrive in Australia as part of his expedition, something future explorers would find invaluable in their explorations.

The Last Frontier focuses on another early pioneer, Australian born Horace Wills, who overcame an extremely challenging childhood and was determined to achieve success as a pastoralist.

Horace was an adventurer who led his own overlanding party into new areas of settlement to the south and south-west of the limits of settlement in New South Wales. He was a man who lived for the challenges that life offered, and he was more successful than most.

Horace's relationship with the Aboriginal people he encountered while he and the other pastoralists were forcing them off their traditional lands reflects the often-fraught interactions of these two vastly different cultures. However, unlike most of his contemporaries, Horace was determined to work alongside rather against the Aboriginal culture and people, an incredibly progressive and positive view for that period of Australian history.

While our history books recount the momentous advances made when Europeans spread across the continent, the stories of Ralph Entwistle, John Horrocks and Horace Wills are a reminder that those advances were almost always built on smaller endeavours, often made by people whose names we rarely hear today.

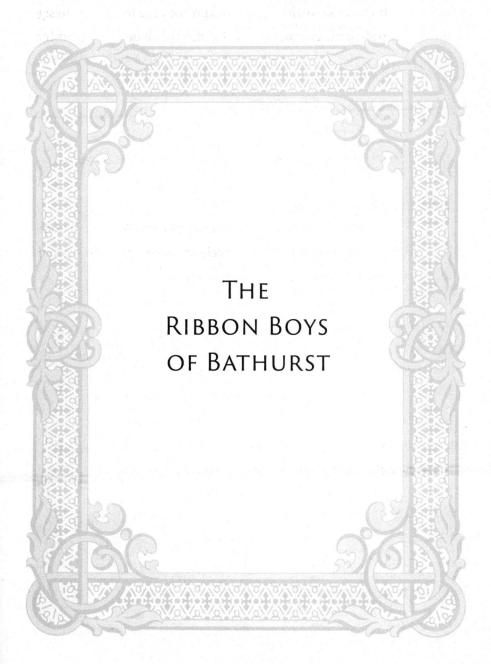

THE
RIBBON BOYS
OF BATHURST

THE LAND BEYOND
THE MOUNTAINS

N ot to put too fine a point on it all, Britain founded Australia as a dumping ground for its exploding population of convicts. Irrespective of arguments over the social, religious, political or economic pressures that led to the soaring conviction rates, Britain had run out of options to house those unfortunates its legal system deemed to be criminals. The loss of their North American colonies and the failure to find suitable alternative sites for convict settlements in West Africa and elsewhere made the European landings up and down the east coast of Australia both timely and inevitable. The same pressures that created those settlements guaranteed they would continue to grow once established.

The largest of those settlements was established at Sydney, on the foreshore of Port Jackson. As the convicts, soldiers and increasing numbers of free settlers sailed into Port Jackson's sheltered anchorage in the first 25 years of what was now the Colony of New South Wales, it became apparent that all who came had entered their own special sort of prison. Captain Arthur Phillip's First Fleet brought just over 1000 Europeans to the Australian continent, with just over three quarters of that number being convicts. Free settlers did not begin arriving until 1793, five years after Phillip, and they arrived at a penal colony still struggling to survive.

There were many attractions in Port Jackson when Phillip arrived. The port itself was one of the finest ships' harbours in the world, the climate was benign, and, through Tank Stream, there was enough water for the early inhabitants of the new colony. The seas seemed full of fish, the bush abounded with a whole new range of animals, and most of those animals were edible. There were some problems with the natives they were displacing, but nothing that a bolt of brightly coloured cloth or the pointy end of a musket couldn't fix.

As the weeks there became months, and the months became years, it became obvious that the soil throughout their little settlement was thin and sandy, and that most of the crops which thrived in England literally struggled to take root in New South Wales. There were rich and productive soils in the hinterland, along the well-watered plains of the Parramatta, Nepean and Hawkesbury Rivers, but much of that land was taken up by well-connected free settlers, many of whom were former British Army officers who had chosen to remain in the colony when their term of service there expired. They tended to look to large-scale pastoralism rather than the small-scale agriculture and horticulture necessary to support the growing population in the Sydney Basin. Were it not for all those kangaroos and all those fish, the colony may not have survived.

There was land to the north and the south of the growing settlement, and that land was quickly gobbled up by both new and established colonists. But that land was also finite, in the sense that the further the settler was from Sydney, the greater the difficulty in fetching supplies and sending produce to market for sale. In an age of limited transportation options, there was also an economic limit to expansion. Movement inland towards the centre of the continent was problematic as the Blue Mountains, the local iteration of the Great Dividing Range, kept the colonists and convicts hemmed in along the coastal littoral. There were ways through and across those mountains, ancient pathways known to generations of Aboriginals, but it was not until 1813 that Europeans were able to find a way across.

Prompted in part by successive drought years in 1812 and 1813, Gregory Blaxland, William Lawson and William Charles Wentworth set out from Blaxland's farm near modern day St. Mary's on 11 May 1813 with four servants and five dogs. Careful planning, which included following ridgelines and not just valley floors, saw the men complete a passage across the mountains in 21 days. On the other side of the mountains they found well-watered grasslands and well-forested hills.

Looking out at just the country he could see from the peak named in his honour, Blaxland believed that this land below would support the Colony of New South Wales for at least 30 years. There was land enough in the west for pastoralists and small farmers, for ticket of leave men — convicts who had been granted conditional pardons — and for the convicts who would be required to clear the land as well.

It was a new frontier, with new challenges but with new possibilities as well. It was also a frontier where the centre of authority would sometimes be a long way distant.

*   *   *

Within a few short weeks of the return of the three explorers, work was underway to build a road across the mountains to the seemingly limitless plains beyond. The first thoroughfare, Cox's Line of Road, would be upgraded and duplicated in the months and years ahead; it had to be, so great was the traffic that used it. Even before it was completed, there was a rush to take up land on those western slopes and plains.

As soon as the nature of the land beyond the mountains became public knowledge, the office of then Governor Lachlan Macquarie was flooded with applications by colonists seeking grants of land in the newly discovered districts. Most of those who applied did so on the basis of their past services to the Crown in either the military field or in some civilian administrative position. Naturally, requests from the more prominent colonists were better received than those from persons further down the colony's social ladder and those who received the earliest grants took up the best available land, generally the well-watered lands alongside the many rivers and streams flowing westwards and south-westwards from the mountains.

Those who applied or arrived later were forced to go either further west, out onto the seemingly endless plains, or further back into the mountains and onto the more marginal farmland further back into the hills and gullies. This "marginal" land was generally far better than the land now available anywhere in the Sydney Basin so it, too, was eagerly sought out. Besides, this was the frontier and one of the rules of life on the frontier was that success was more often a function of hard work and diligence than it was of choosing the best land available and expecting to be successful on that basis alone.

A second rule was that the trappings of a civilised society always followed some distance behind the pioneers. This remained the rule west of the mountains where most of the land in the Bathurst district had been taken up and was being worked before Bathurst itself came into existence.

*　　*　　*

In May 1815, at the terminus of Cox's Line of Road, Governor Lachlan Macquarie ordered the Union Jack raised on a temporary flagpole, listened and watched as his military honour guard fired a single volley and then declared that the settlement which would grow on that spot would be named Bathurst after the Secretary of State for War and the Colonies, Henry Bathurst. For most of the next decade, the little village that occupied that site was known simply as "The Settlement", and it served primarily as a jumping off point for inland explorers and as a meeting place for the district's established and would-be settlers.

In that decade, Bathurst consisted of little more than a few government buildings near the Bathurst River. One of those buildings was a solid brick courthouse, a building which also contained living quarters for both the Police Magistrate and the Government Medical Officer posted to the district. Other buildings constructed during those early years included a gaol, a women's' factory and a Government House — a cottage in all but name — where the Governor stayed whenever he visited the settlement.

Bathurst, with its surrounding farms and farmlets, was a frontier town, a precarious little outpost of Great Britain perched at the very edge of the limits of civilization, occupying lands whose former inhabitants did not always respond peacefully to their dispossession. Their responses took many forms, from simply moving away when that was practicable, to the theft of stock and any other items left lying around, to the spearing of stock and the killing of isolated shepherds and farm labourers. In return, the European colonists' responses to these depredations were characteristically disproportionate to the threat actually posed.

For several months in 1824, martial law was in effect throughout the Bathurst district. Troops were despatched from Sydney to enforce that law and the most belligerent of the Aboriginal leaders hounded and harassed until they were forced to accept an imposed settlement.

As the threat posed by dispossessed and marginalised Aboriginals receded, another threat began to manifest itself, that of bushrangers or as they were most commonly described at that time, absconders. The frontier that the settlers were pushing up against offered a sanctuary of sorts to those who found either convict servitude or the restraints of colonial society too confining. Those who sought to evade those strictures went bush, and in that bush travelled far and wide in their efforts to remain free and to support themselves. By ranging widely through the bush, these absconders earned the new sobriquet of bushrangers.

To address the new threats that emerged at the edges of settlement, a new paramilitary force was also called into existence, the New South Wales Mounted Police.

*   *   *

The first detachment of the mounted police was formed at the direction of the then governor, Sir Thomas Brisbane, in 1824, partly in response to a series of attacks undertaken by Aboriginals in the Bathurst district. Peace came to that part of the frontier after several months of martial law and the signing of a peace treaty with the local tribes. The mounted police were recognised as making a significant contribution to this outcome and there were calls for them to become a permanent force operating at the outer limits of settlement.

The New South Wales Mounted Police was established as a permanent police force in September 1825 with an authorised strength of two officers, two sergeants and 20 privates. The first source of recruits for the new force was the British Army infantry regiment then serving in New South Wales. Those earliest recruits were men who had been discharged from the regiment, but they were soon joined by a steady stream of secondees. Army officers were never obliged to serve with the mounted police. Many did, but they had all volunteered for that duty. To overcome the paucity of good horses suitable for service with the new unit, the government made a large purchase of horses in 1827. It also ordered Government Farms, such as those at Bathurst and Wellington, to set aside part of their produce as forage for the mounted police.

The New South Wales Mounted Police were first based at Bathurst, which had been the epicentre for Aboriginal resistance to colonial expansion in that area and which was also becoming something of a magnet for runaway convicts. The police were in action early in 1826 when, under the command of Lieutenant Thomas Evernden, they clashed with a band of absconders known as Sullivan's Gang in March of that year. Four months later, in July, Evernden and his men received high praise from the colony's new governor, Sir Ralph Darling himself, after they had captured seven runaway convicts who had been moving westerly through the district, travelling with a number of stolen horses, cattle and general provisions.

The success of the mounted police was such that it grew almost exponentially. By 1829 the force was commanded by a Lieutenant Colonel Snodgrass, who was based in Sydney, while its area of operations was now divided into districts. The main frontier area was designated the Western District, and it in turn was then subdivided into three divisions. The First Division, based at Bathurst, was under the command of Lieutenant James Brown of the 57th Regiment of Foot. The other two divisions were based at Newcastle and Goulburn. In 1830 a number of changes were made to the force's command structure. Captain Charles Forbes of the 39th (Dorsetshire) Regiment was placed in command of the whole force while a young Scotsman, Lieutenant Lachlan Macalister, took command of the Goulburn District.

*   *   *

In its first decade of existence, Bathurst was subject to most of the problems associated with the Australian frontier: weather, the tyranny of distance, and all the little and large inconveniences that confront pioneers everywhere. One problem, which was more an annoyance than a cause for major concern, was runaway convicts joining up with like-minded men to form bands of bushrangers. There were several reasons for this. One main one was that, inasmuch as there were gradations present in the convict ranks, the Bathurst district was populated by a "superior" class of convict.

Originally, most of the farm labourers in the district were either ticket of leave men or they were about to become ticket of leave men. This ticket of leave was a form of parole granted to well-behaved convicts, usually after two or three years' work as an assigned servant. The ticket came with some restrictions: a ticket of leave holder was expected to report regularly to authorities and freedom of movement was often curtailed to prevent an exodus of workers from any particular district. A ticket of leave was halfway to a full parole and allowed its bearer to work for wages rather than just food and lodging. It was something most convicts worked hard to obtain and to retain because tickets of leave could be, and often were, revoked for any involvement in criminal activity.

Those superior convicts and ex-convicts were gradually supplanted from around 1820 onwards as they either moved elsewhere with their masters or moved on themselves when they received a full pardon, something which appeared to have taken only a few years from the time a ticket of leave was granted.

The nature of pastoralism around Bathurst also changed with the coming of the new decade. A second wave of settlers arrived to try to make a living from the rich lands in the district. A number of those who had originally been granted land in the west had never intended to either live or farm there; for them, the land grant was an investment for the future when increased land prices would mean a tidy little return on investment. They were more than happy to sell parcels of land to the settlers who continued to move out from Sydney and elsewhere. Those settlers either brought with them their own assigned servants or applied for some soon after they arrived in the Bathurst district. These assigned servants were usually not from the superior class.

Other factors also contributed to a significant increase in the number of bushrangers who became active along the outer limits of settlement, which contained the Hunter Valley as well as Bathurst, Goulburn and Wellington. One was that the geography of those outer limits became better known to the population at large, through newspaper reporting and the usual practices of commerce. Instead of the great unknown, absconders now literally had maps to guide them in their escape and specific escape routes and potential hiding places could now be identified before the event.

A second factor was the virtual removal of the Aboriginal threat along the borders of settlement in those regions after December 1824. Whereas escape into the bush meant almost certain death from either starvation or Aboriginal spears before then, the defeat of the resisting and marauding Aboriginals around Bathurst and the virtual extermination of the Aboriginal population elsewhere removed one of the major threats to the survival of an absconder in the bush.

Finally, there was a significant increase in the number of firearms in the frontier areas. As well as providing protection from possible attacks by hostile Aboriginals, firearms were also sometimes the only providers of food in a harsh environment. As more firearms came into the areas for the right reasons, they became as well more readily available for the wrong purposes. An unarmed absconder and a heavily armed bushranger pose two very different levels of threat.

*   *   *

The best-known and most feared in this first iteration of Australian bushrangers was John Donohoe, later popularised as the Wild Colonial Boy, "Bold" Jack Donahue. Donohoe and his gang of up to a dozen men were at large and raided across the Liverpool, Windsor and Penrith districts for four years after Donohoe absconded from service in 1825. After the gang committed a series of armed robberies against both travellers and homesteads, a reward of one hundred pounds was offered for the capture of Donohoe and for his lieutenant, a free settler named Underwood who had joined the gang of his own volition. Should their killer/captor be a convict, a ticket of leave would be included as part of the reward.

Arrested once, Donohoe escaped from custody and was regarded by many, and especially among the ex-convict population, as leading a charmed life. A police sharpshooter killed Donohoe after a carefully staged ambush, but his main co-offenders, runaway convicts named Webber and Walmsley, both escaped. The two were later captured while attempting to rob a mail coach. Walmsley turned King's Evidence and was later exiled to Van Diemen's Land; Webber was hanged.

The destruction of Donohoe's gang did not end the bushranger threat. His example was thought to have the potential to inspire others to also go bush, particularly if they viewed themselves as victims of the social system in both their home country and New South Wales rather than as the common criminals who most of them were. For the over-whelmingly English and Anglican landowners, there was also the thinly veiled threat posed by the large numbers of Irish Catholic convicts with their inbred distrust of the English. Add to this the ever-expanding set-tlement with its ever-expanding frontier, and it was obvious that there would be an ongoing role for the mounted police wherever a convict-based system and the borderland between civilization and wilderness co-existed.

The *Sydney Gazette* of 9 September 1825 noted, in passing, that mounted police horse patrols had been formed in the Newcastle and Bathurst districts. It did not mention, because it had not yet been announced, that Lieutenant Thomas Evernden of the 3rd Regiment of Foot would command the detachment based at Bathurst. This was an appointment whose repercussions would for a short time later dominate the settlement at Bathurst.

Thomas Evernden was born in Kent, England, in 1788, the same year that a permanent European settlement was established in New South Wales. Joining the British Army as a lieutenant, Evernden's regiment, also known as the East Kent regiment or "The Buffs", arrived in Sydney aboard the *Royal Charlotte* in April 1825 for a three-year posting to the colony. In December of that year, Evernden was seconded to the mounted police and given command of the detachment based at Bathurst. Evernden apparently enjoyed the position; if nothing else, it gave him a status and an authority that he could probably never have achieved in England.

When his regiment was recalled from its service in New South Wales, Evernden resigned his commission and opted to remain in the colony. In 1828, he was appointed Police Magistrate and Superintendent of Police at Bathurst, an area he now considered to be his home and his destiny. From Governor Ralph Darling he received a land grant of 2560 acres just outside Bathurst. The property was known as Bartlett's, located in the area called Wimbledon, and it was here that he built an impressive country homestead which he named Littlebourne, presumably after the village of the same name near Canterbury in Kent.

In 1827, Evernden married Elizabeth Kelson, who unfortunately passed away two years later. When he remarried in January 1830, his new wife was Mary Jane Hawkins, the daughter of a former captain in the Royal Navy who had become superintendent of the convicts at Bathurst.

If Evernden and his mounted police ever needed assistance to cope with Aboriginal, bushrangers or any form of natural catastrophe, he could call upon the military for assistance. There was no regimental headquarters in Bathurst, the nearest one being at Parramatta, however, there was usually a detachment of soldiers based there, commanded by either a captain or a major from whichever regiment was then stationed in New South Wales. From 1827 to 1830, that regiment was the 57th (West Middlesex) Regiment of Foot which, with its commanding officer, Lieutenant Colonel C.W. Wall, was primarily based in and around Sydney.

*   *   *

By the time Thomas Evernden arrived in Bathurst, the pastoral nature of the district was beginning to take shape. Many of those who were originally granted land in the area, men like the Reverend Samuel Marsden, had either not taken up their runs or had sold them either outright or in packages. A second wave of settlers moved into the district from the early 1820s, and these included many men and women who were determined to tame the bush, make the land productive and establish a place on that land for future generations of their family. One such settler was George Suttor.

Suttor's interest in the colony of New South Wales had been piqued by a series of meetings with Sir Joseph Banks in England. Convinced that his future lay in the colony, Suttor emigrated as a free settler and took up land at Baulkham Hills near Parramatta, where he introduced a range of fruit and vegetables that Banks had believed would thrive in the new colony. They mostly did, so Suttor continued to experiment with other foodstuffs, wine and anything he thought might have a useful future. He also became close friends with Governor William Bligh, taking his friend's side in Bligh's ongoing disputes with the officers of the New South Wales Corps, the military guardians of the colony. When Bligh was arrested and sent back to England, Suttor followed his friend and gave evidence before the various trials and enquiries that followed.

Back in New South Wales, and several years later, George Suttor applied for a land grant in the Bathurst region and, in 1822, set out from Parramatta to cross the mountains to the Bathurst Plains. As well as several assigned servants, Suttor was accompanied by his third son, William, who had been born on the family property at Baulkham Hills in 1805. The Suttor's and their men drove 400 sheep, several cattle and a number of horses ahead of them. For some reason, their expected land grant did not eventuate, so they took up a modest holding of 320 acres at Brucedale, a few miles from Bathurst. Over the next decade, they built up from this small start, and as the 1820's drew to a close, the Suttor's Brucedale property covered 10,000 acres and was a place where most forms of agriculture and horticulture were being practiced successfully.

Another prominent Bathurst Plains settler was George Ranken, a Scotsman from Ayrshire, who first sailed to Hobart as a free settler, arriving there in October 1821. Neither Ranken nor his wife, Janet, was particularly taken by their prospects for advancement in Van Diemen's Land, and they soon relocated to Sydney. There, the Ranken's rented 2000 acres at Petersham and, in association with a cheese maker from Cheshire, soon established an extremely successful cheese making business.

In 1822, the New South Wales government announced that it would begin granting 2000 acre lots in the Bathurst district to those who were prepared to work those lots. George and Janette Ranken were among the first to take advantage of the offer and selected a property for themselves which they named Kelloshiel. They also selected properties on behalf of two of their business associates. For Thomas Icely, they selected a run which he would call Saltram, and for Captain John Piper, who owned the land they rented at Petersham, they selected a property that he would call Alloway Bank.

George and Janet Ranken set out for their land grant as soon as it was approved, taking their newborn child with them in a wagon. The state of the tracks through the mountains meant that a trip that is today completed in just a few hours took the Ranken's all of two weeks. With their arrival in Bathurst, Janet Ranken became just the third European woman to journey to the western side of the Great Dividing Range. The other two were the wife of Thomas Hawkins, the local superintendent of convicts, and the wife of the manager of the Government Farm at Bathurst.

George's nephew, Arthur Ranken, arrived from Scotland in 1826, and worked with George and Janet at Kelloshiel for several years. By the late 1820's, land further out to the west — the vast western plains of New South Wales — was being opened up to settlers. Arthur Ranken acquired a station he named Glen Logan on the Lachlan River, and George also acquired a 4,000-acre run nearby. Arthur was despatched to manage both properties while George, Janet and their growing family remained at Kelloshiel.

Finally, another free settler who would figure prominently in Bathurst's early history was John Liscombe. Liscombe had arrived in New South Wales as an emigrant in 1825 and just a few months later had taken up a run he named Rock Forest, almost 20 kilometres to the south-west of Bathurst. Like several other pastoralists in the district, Liscombe was also appointed to a number of official positions in the administration of the area's civil affairs. In 1827, he was made Coroner for the Bathurst district, and the following year he was also appointed Postmaster and Clerk to the Bench of Magistrates who sat at Bathurst. All were positions he would hold for the next decade.

Again, like most of the free settlers who took up land in the Bathurst district, several convicts were assigned to John Liscombe at his Rock Forest run. One of them destined to achieve a certain kind of fame was Ralph Entwistle.

Entwistle was a pleasant looking young man from Bolton in Lancashire. At 175 centimetres in height, he was a little taller than average, with grey eyes, sandy coloured hair and a ruddy, freckled complexion. Back home in Bolton, he had worked his trade as a brick maker, but in 1827 he was convicted on a charge of stealing clothing and sentenced to transportation for life to New South Wales. Entwistle was 25 years old when he arrived in Sydney on 18 March 1828, one of 189 prisoners aboard the convict transport *John*.

Shortly after he arrived in the colony, Entwistle was assigned to work on John Liscombe's farm near Bathurst. From all reports, Entwistle was a steady, reliable and diligent worker, so much so that Liscombe had recommended that Entwistle be granted a ticket of leave well ahead of when such a release would normally be given. Then everything suddenly went wrong.

THE ABSCONDERS

In November 1829, John Liscombe entrusted two of his assigned servants with what was an important task, to take Rock Forest's wool clip to Sydney by bullock dray and there deposit it with Liscombe's agent for either local sale or export to England. While in Sydney, the men were also to call into several merchant houses to collect the provisions and supplies that Liscombe had already ordered.

Given that both men were convicted criminals who were still working out their sentences of transportation for life, it may have appeared almost foolhardy for Liscombe to have entrusted them with such a task. However, assigned convicts still outnumbered free labourers at that time, so it was commonplace throughout the settled districts of New South Wales for most of the work like this to be undertaken by the convicts.

Although neither in prison nor in chains, these assignees were still limited in their freedom of movement, and if they chose to attempt an escape, there were few options open to them. Within the limits of settlement, they would soon be recognised and caught as their descriptions were widely circulated in colonial newspapers. If they fled beyond those limits, they faced the real chance of death by starvation or death at the hands of the Aboriginals who roamed through the bush there. To survive, they would need to become bushrangers, part of a larger band, and even the most successful of these, John Donohoe, had eventually been hunted down and killed by the authorities.

Such considerations would not have distracted John Liscombe or his two assigned men either. Liscombe was regarded as a fair master, which meant that he kept his assigned men in reasonable quarters, fed them reasonable food and expected a reasonable amount of work in return. Unlike some masters, Liscombe did not have his men dragged before a magistrate for the slightest infraction of rules or the slightest sign of insubordination. Besides, Liscombe was reasonably confident in the fidelity of the men he had despatched with his precious wool clip. One has never been identified, but was most probably William Gahan, an Irishman who had been with Liscombe for more than a year now. The second was Ralph Entwistle, and he had made himself so useful to Liscombe that the pastoralist had just recently lodged the paperwork necessary for Entwistle to be granted a conditional pardon, the Ticket of Leave.

That paperwork had been lodged with Thomas Evernden and it was probable that, sometime in the new year of 1830, Evernden would sign the papers and forward them to the Governor's secretary in Sydney. Soon afterwards, Entwistle would be well on his way to becoming a free man again.

*   *   *

For the two convicts, the trip home was nearly over. They were approaching the ford across the Macquarie River just below Bathurst and thought they would have more than enough time to make it back to Rock Forest before dark and, if they didn't, they would just find a suitable spot and camp there for the night. Besides, it was very hot and both man and animal now needed a break from the killer sun. Entwistle led the bullock team off the road and into some shade beneath the gum trees that lined it. Then he and his companion did something that neither had probably done since boyhood; they took off all their clothes and threw them into a pile before jumping into the cool waters of the river, washing off several days' worth of dirt and dust and behaving as though they didn't have a worry in the world.

The two young men had only been in the water for a few minutes when, above the sound of their own voices and the splashing, they heard the unmistakable sound of many horses approaching from the direction of Bathurst. Thinking quickly, they pushed themselves into a bed of reeds at the river's edge and looked back towards the ford. As they looked, several horsemen in uniform appeared and splashed across the river. They were obviously an escort, because they wore army uniforms and immediately behind them came an impressive-looking carriage with at least two people inside. The coat of arms on the door indicated that those occupants were the Governor, Sir Ralph Darling, and his wife.

The vice-regal couple and their escort were soon out of sight, and the men were certain they hadn't been spotted. As they left the water to collect their clothes and dress themselves, a second group of uniformed horsemen trotted down to and across the ford. This time, the convicts were certainly seen, as the leading horseman called out to them and then led his small group across to where the two men were now hurriedly dressing. They may or may not have recognised the leading horseman as Lieutenant Thomas Evernden, Police Magistrate and head of the mounted police at Bathurst. Although he was part of the Governor's escort, Evernden had no doubt about where his duty lay.

Evernden directed his men to immediately arrest Entwistle and his companion and take them back to the cells at the Bathurst lockup. He next saw them when they appeared before him in court on charges that

Evernden himself had laid. Both men were charged with "causing an affront to the Governor and his party". Evidence was led detailing the circumstances surrounding the incident and the arrests, but no evidence was offered as to whether or not Sir Ralph Darling or his wife had even seen the men in the river or, if they had, either or both had been affronted by what they had seen. It probably would not have mattered anyway. The charges were Evernden's, the courtroom was Evernden's and the verdict and sentence were Evernden's.

Both men were found guilty, and both men were sentenced to 50 lashes, to be publicly administered by the flagellator appointed for the purpose. In addition, the application for a Ticket of Leave to be granted to Ralph Entwistle was denied before it had even been formally submitted and he was given to believe that it would be a long time before another application would be considered. It was a high price to pay for trying to cool down on a hot day.

*   *   *

Fifty lashes from a whip known as a "cat o' nine tails" would lacerate the skin and cause intense pain. For some of those about to undergo such a punishment, a kind of relief could be gained by slipping a small amount of money to the flagellator to encourage him to deliver lighter strokes than might otherwise be delivered. If no such inducement was offered, if the flagellator was in a mean mood or if his performance was being monitored, he might lay on with a heavy hand, the lead-tipped tails of the cat not just breaking the skin but biting into the fatty tissue and muscle below. Fifty lashes were often far more than was necessary to expose the ribs and even the spine itself.

Over a few weeks, the tissue and torn flesh would heal, leaving a complex network of scars, or "stripes" as the convicts called them. These were not only a permanent reminder of what had occurred but also a warning of what might be administered again for any future recalcitrance. The physical wounds healed into scars; the mental wounds could become something else altogether.

* * *

Ralph Entwistle would neither forgive nor forget what had occurred through the sheer arrogance and bloody-mindedness of Thomas Evernden, but he would learn to bide his time. He would also use that time carefully and productively, to seek out like-minded fellows, convicts like himself who had been let down by a capricious penal system that lifted a few up but dragged many, many more down. Any faith he may have had in the system, any belief that a person such as himself could rise up in society had been stripped away with the same precision that the skin on his back had been stripped away by the cat o'nine tails. He would strike back at the system, but it would be at a time, in a place and by a method which would make plain to everyone just what men like Evernden could bring out in others.

He would take his time, and he would be careful, too. There rarely was honour among thieves in a society such as this, and he knew there were many of his fellow convicts working as assigned servants who would willingly reveal any plans he might make to the authorities in the belief that such a revelation would earn them a reduction in their own sentence and perhaps even a ticket of leave. So, Ralph Entwistle looked around with great care and only approached those men he thought might be willing to fight — and most likely die — in order to balance some parts of a ledger that had been so heavily weighted against them.

William Gahan, especially if he was the other man flogged alongside

Entwistle, would have been one of the early confidantes. At 24 years, Gahan was just one year younger than the Englishman, and the two were not dissimilar physically. Both were around 175 centimetres in height and well-built, with Entwistle's sandy hair and grey eyes a contrast to Gahan's brown hair and brown eyes. Like so many other convicts, Gahan was an Irishman, a simple ploughman from Tipperary, albeit one convicted of six armed robberies and one whose death sentence had been commuted to transportation for life. Gahan was also illiterate, having never attended school in his life, and a relatively recent arrival, landing in Sydney from the *Eliza II* in June 1829. Within days of his arrival he was assigned to John Luscombe, had met Ralph Entwistle and was now one of Entwistle's closest friends and confederates.

Another of Liscombe's assigned servants trusted completely by both men was Michael Kearney. Aged 23 years and, like Gahan, a semi-literate ploughman from Tipperary, Kearney had arrived in New South Wales in January 1829 aboard the convict transport *Governor Ready,* which had carried 200 Irish convicts direct from Cork in Ireland to Sydney. Also aboard the *Governor Ready* was the 24-year-old John Kenny, a carter from Cork who also followed Kearney out to John Liscombe's farm. He, too, became part of the group coalescing around Ralph Entwistle.

Although there were several other assigned servants at Rock Forest, there was only one other who was brought completely into what was becoming a conspiracy. His name was John Shepherd, and he was a 24-year-old boatman from Wiltshire in England. Another recent arrival, Shepherd had landed in Sydney in August 1829 and was sent down to John Liscombe's farm a few days later.

To build their numbers, the group would have to recruit volunteers from other farms and, given the outcome to be expected, this process was very carefully undertaken, with an approach made only when there was some indication that the individual was at least trustworthy. One of the first outsiders approached was Patrick Gleeson, a 28-year-old labourer from Tipperary who arrived in New South Wales in the second half of 1829.

Gleeson had been assigned to a farm owned by a Mr. C. T. Ware near Bathurst and it was there, too, that one other member of the group was recruited. This was Thomas Dunne, at 33 years, one of the oldest convicts who would join Entwistle. Dunne was a widower and a shepherd who had been sentenced to transportation for life for house robbery, and who had arrived aboard the *Sophia* in 1829.

Rounding out the core of what would become Entwistle's gang was another Irishman and two Englishmen. The Irishman was Dominick Daley, a 32-year-old ploughman, married with four children, who was transported for life in 1828 for stealing a horse in his native Armagh. Arriving in New South Wales aboard the convict transport *Fergusson* in 1829, he was assigned to the farm of a Mr. Johnson near Bathurst.

The two Englishmen were James Driver, a 22-year-old brick maker from Boston in Lincolnshire, and Robert Webster, a 28-year-old waterman from Epping. Driver had arrived in 1829 and was assigned to a free settler named Lambert at Bathurst while Webster, who had arrived two years earlier in 1827, was assigned to Thomas Evernden at Bartlett's. It was probably this fact more than anything else that brought Webster into Entwistle's little group of conspirators. Those conspirators — Entwistle included — do not appear to have drawn up any grand plan for what they were going to do. Rather, it seems as though they simply planned to abscond en masse, repay some old debts, and see how their little adventure played itself out.

*   *   *

Sometime towards the end of September 1830, Ralph Entwistle and his eight companions simply rode away from their assigned farms, taking whatever weapons and rations they could lay their hands on. With that simple action, they moved from being convicts to being absconders. It was a short transition and within another short time, they went from being absconders to being bushrangers.

The absconders would have made a pre-arranged meeting spot and may even have cached weapons and food there. Wherever that meeting place was — most probably in the bush to the south-west of Bathurst — it was here that further plans were hatched. At least one of those present, Michael Gahan, had knowledge of and probable involvement in the Whiteboys and Ribbonmen movements in Ireland. Both of these 19th-century movements involved the rural Catholic underclass, who directed their sometimes violent protests and sabotage against the Protestant, English or Anglophile landowning class. The earlier Whiteboys and the later Ribbonmen wore distinctive ribbons, sometimes white and sometimes green, as part symbol and part uniform. Entwistle and his little group decided that attaching white ribbons to their hats would be a message too obvious to ignore.

Early on the morning of Thursday 23 September 1830, Ralph Entwistle rode at the head of eight heavily armed men into the main space between the various buildings which made up the homestead at Bartlett's, Thomas Evernden's farm just outside Bathurst. Brandishing a pistol and calling out at the top of his voice, Entwistle directed everyone present to come out of the buildings. Only a couple came out of the main house in the complex, and from them Entwistle learned that neither Mr nor Mrs Evernden were present, nor were they expected home that day.

Several men had emerged from the huts which formed another part of the farmstead, and Entwistle now turned to speak to them. Although he knew most by sight, and most of them knew him and his companions as well, he still introduced himself and outlined what they all hoped might now happen: some form of general uprising which might end, if they were all united, in better conditions for them all. If not, New South Wales was a very large colony, and who knew where they might all finish up. "Join us," he called, and looked carefully at them, meeting their gazes as he looked from one man to the next.

One man stood alone at the front of his small hut, saying nothing. His name was John Greenwood, but for some reason he preferred to be called either James or Jim. He was Thomas Evernden's overseer, and most present knew him as such, by reputation if not be name. After Entwistle called on all the assigned men to join him in freedom, and while he waited for some indication of what they were likely to do, he turned to Greenwood and said that they would even accept such a man as him. The implication was clear, and Greenwood responded in kind, saying he would not be joining them, and saying it in a tone of voice which made obvious his contempt for Entwistle and the others.

Rising to the challenge, Entwistle looked down at Greenwood from his horse and said to the overseer that, if what he had just said was really what he meant, he, Entwistle, felt inclined to shoot him. All was silent now, with everyone looking at these two men who now clearly hated one another and who were equally engaged in a battle of wills.

Greenwood didn't look away. He said simply as he looked from one to another of the mounted men, that none of those present were game to shoot him. As if to emphasise the point, he opened the front of his shirt and pointed to a spot just above his heart.

Two shots rang out, so close together that the second seemed to be almost an echo of the first. Entwistle and Michael Gahan had responded simultaneously to Greenwood's challenge. All eyes swivelled from their still-smoking pistols to James Greenwood, who had been knocked backwards by the impact of the bullets, both of which had struck him in the chest. He gasped, "Oh, Lord," and in a slow and painful pantomime tried to walk back through the door into his hut. It was not a walk though, it was a stagger; a series of jerky movements, and it seemed as though his legs were about to give way underneath him. He reached out towards the door post and, as he did so, a third shot struck him squarely in the middle of the back.

Michael Kearney lowered his pistol, and watched as Greenwood slumped to the ground, folding in upon himself rather than falling outright. Greenwood seemed to understand that he was now lying on the ground as he stretched his arms and legs as if trying to find a more comfortable resting position. He had not said anything, nor had he made a noise of any kind since the pistol shots rang out. Now, his chest rose and fell once, then again before all movement stopped and the man was dead.

Perhaps sensing that the moment could be slipping away, Entwistle turned and called across to the assembled men, asking whether those present were all of the assigned servants on the property. One of them answered that, yes, all the convicts were present. Entwistle again asked if any of the men were willing to ride away with him. After a pause, two men stepped forward, one of them being the man who had just answered Entwistle's question. Entwistle told the two assignees to take whatever they wanted from Greenwood's room and be ready to leave almost immediately. They did just that, stepping carefully over Greenwood's body to enter and exit the little hut.

*   *   *

The scene which played out at Thomas Evernden's farm was repeated at many other farms across the district in the coming days. At every farm the armed men raided, the theme and the actions were almost identical, with one exception. The kind of foolhardy bravery which James Greenwood had displayed was not repeated, nor was the fatal violence which had followed Greenwood's provocation. If anything,

Entwistle and his men assumed an almost benign approach to the raising of rebellion.

One of their earliest victims was a free labourer, a ticket of leave man employed by George Suttor at Brucedale. Early one afternoon, possibly the same day as the raid on Evernden's, this man was returning home when he was bailed up by Entwistle's gang at a local feature known as One Tree Hill. The bushrangers firstly admired the man's clothes, and then insisted that he take them off and hand them over. When the poor labourer arrived back at Brucedale just on dusk, George Suttor at first thought that the near-naked man had gone insane.

At one of the first homesteads they raided, located on the Vale Road and owned by a man named Johnstone, one of the assigned servants informed Entwistle that Johnstone was a good master to work for, and also that Johnstone's wife was very ill. Entwistle told his men to take anything of value from the outbuildings, but they were not to enter the homestead. It was a direction followed by all.

From Johnstone's farm, the gang headed to the Dunn's Plain area, directly south of Bathurst. In a little over four hours there, they raided farms belonging to John Brown, Sampson Sealy and Watson Steel, before continuing over some hills to another valley filled with isolated homesteads on half-cleared farms. At Thomas Icely's farm, Saltram, they made themselves a meal and then left without causing any real damage. Next, they rode a relatively short distance to a property owned by a man named Bettington where they took some horses but nothing else. These were exceptions to what quickly became a general rule: at each property they raided, the gang would steal food, horses, guns and ammunition. They would also attempt to recruit new members for the gang using a blend of threats and flattery, so they departed most of the farms they raided with more men than when they arrived.

There may have been a little more organisation to the rebellion than appeared to be the case. As well as the convicts who were assigned to free settlers, there were also convicts on government service in and around Bathurst. Some worked on the Government Farm established there, but many more were engaged on the various public infrastructure and public building programs that were being undertaken west of the mountains, and especially in Bathurst itself. To replace the ford where Ralph Entwistle had come to grief, a bridge was being built over the Macquarie River. The convicts building the bridge were known as the "Bathurst Bridge Party" and five of them — Joseph Gladman, Thomas Gray, Thomas Hodges, John Scott and Martin Mangon (also known as Manning) — absconded in a group to join Entwistle. At least three of the five had been transported to New South Wales aboard convict ships carrying other key members of Entwistle's gang.

As well as being regarded as the richest and most successful of all the Bathurst pastoralists, George Ranken seems to have generally been regarded as a good master to be assigned to, and yet he lost two of his men to Ralph Entwistle. James Green and George Mole were both Englishmen, were both 19 years of age, and had both travelled to New South Wales aboard the convict transport *John,* alongside Ralph Entwistle.

As is usually the way, the early news of a disturbance among the convict population, of numbers of absconders and outrageous deeds was spread by the bush telegraph and the further the stories travelled, the less accurate they became. The murder of James Greenwood occurred during the morning of 23 September, when Entwistle and the others had been "out" for no longer than two days. By the end of the next day, the gang had held up no more than half a dozen homesteads, with several more to follow the next day. At most of those farms there were only a small number of assigned convicts — half a dozen would have been a large number — and not all of them chose to depart with Entwistle. At its largest, late in the afternoon of Saturday 25 September, the total number of men in the gang may have been as high as 50 but reports of double and triple that number were commonplace.

As well as the stories circulating in the Bathurst district, the news of what was now being called a rebellion or an uprising by numbers of convicts rapidly reached Sydney. Because the information was sketchy and often contradictory, no early official response was made. To help clear up the confusion, George Suttor wrote and despatched several letters over the following days, including one to the editor of the *Sydney Gazette*, a young free-born man named Horatio Wills. In the letter, Suttor said that a small party of bushrangers, numbering just six or eight, had risen at two farms near Bathurst. At both farms they had armed themselves and also forced other men at those farms, both convict and free, to join them.

In what was a somewhat breathless style, Suttor went on to relate what happened when Entwistle's men arrived at Brucedale. He said that, by then, there may have been 80 of them, and because of those overwhelming numbers they were able to take all but one of his men. The decision to leave that one man was quite deliberate; the man was a shepherd, and Entwistle understood that the Suttors would require assistance with their sheep at that time of the year. Suttor also revealed that Entwistle and his gang said that they meant him no harm as he was not considered to be a bad master. Concluding, though, he did note that the bushrangers did remove most of his tea, sugar and tobacco as well as a number of blankets.

On the basis of these eyewitness accounts and the various rumours that were circulating throughout the colony, the various newspapers in the various centres of population offered estimates of the numbers of rebels/absconders that varied from as low as 50 to as high as 500. One even offered the very specific figure of 134. There was also a serious commentary on how many free-born young men had chosen to take up arms with the convicts. It was suggested that, like those convicts, those young, free men wanted a whole raft of restrictions lifted, although no-one seemed able to identify just what those restrictions were. Sitting along such commentaries were reports claiming that the bushranging gang had collected so much "bounty" that the loot was becoming too heavy to carry and was now being secreted in hidden bush dumps.

*　　*　　*

The truth was a long way from what was being reported. While there may have been 50 or more assigned convicts "freed" by Entwistle and his band, most of those thus emancipated were equally prepared to surrender that freedom if the opportunity arose. Those who worked on farms for reasonable men knew that two or three years of honest toil would result in their being granted a Ticket of Leave. Being charged as an absconder could add several more years to that process. The murder of Greenwood was a further complication, because no one could be certain that there would not be further murders. Under the laws of the day, if you were part of a group engaged in criminal activity, you were guilty of all crimes that group committed even if you took no direct part in the crime. This meant that all of Entwistle's men present at Greenwood's death were as guilty of murder as the three men who actually shot him.

Many of those who volunteered to join the band entertained second thoughts once they had given themselves the time and space to really appreciate what it was they were doing. Some would slip away whenever the gang stopped for a break. They would go singly or in pairs as the opportunity arose, but they would certainly go. By the early afternoon of Saturday 25 September, the band probably numbered just a couple of dozen, down from the 50 or so who had ridden into their campsite the previous evening.

Ralph Entwistle was always a realist, and clearly understood what was happening. At some point during that Saturday afternoon, he called his band together and told them that they were all volunteers. He also said that it had never been his intention to compel people to join them; anyone who wasn't comfortable remaining with them was free to leave. At their evening meal that day, Ralph Entwistle sat down to eat with just 14 companions. It was a small group, but it was a group that was well-armed and determined. That determination and those arms would shortly be tested by the forces of law and order who were slowly organising themselves to address the threat that these absconders represented.

THE BATTLE OF GROVE CREEK

T he police and military resources available to confront and control the convict uprising were limited and scattered across a wide region. In Bathurst itself, Lieutenant Thomas Evernden, in his capacity as commander of the mounted police based there, could call on just six troopers. There was a military presence as well, under the command of Major Donald Macpherson of the 39th (Dorsetshire) Regiment, and they would be quickly drawn into the crisis that was unfolding. The troops that Macpherson commanded were limited in numbers — a company at best — and most were engaged in convict-related duties, supervising road gangs and the like. Releasing them from those duties to track down Entwistle and his gang was fraught with the danger of allowing even more prisoners to abscond.

The authorities in Bathurst — civil, police and military — remained of the belief that the bushranger numbers were well in excess of 50, meaning that the Bathurst military and police would probably be out-numbered and outgunned in any clash they had with Entwistle. Urgent requests for assistance were despatched to Sydney and Goulburn. Additional mounted police were sent from Sydney under the command of Lieutenant James Brown, formerly of the 57th Regiment. Brown had previously served in the Bathurst district and knew the area well. Another company of the 39th Regiment was also despatched from Sydney under the command of Captain Horatio Walpole. Leaving their Sydney barracks on Sunday 26 September, they would march directly to Bathurst. No-one was certain when they would arrive. That same day, another troop of mounted police set out from Goulburn under the command of Lieutenant Lachlan Macalister. Time and space were now of the utmost importance.

*   *   *

It seems that Ralph Entwistle and his gang were content to remain in the areas they had come to know, particularly the heavily forested mountains and valleys to the south and south-west of Bathurst. For them, there would not be long rides along the frontier to strike in new and unexpected areas. Nor would there be the splitting up of their little band, the run for individual cover with a new name and a new history and a new chance at life somewhere in New South Wales or beyond. Instead, they would choose to stay together and remain in the same area where they had first made their bid for freedom.

While they remained at large, Entwistle and his men constantly kept an eye out for features such as comfortable hiding places and strongpoints that they could fall back onto, should that ever prove necessary. One place they visited on several occasions was located in a fairly inaccessible area in the criss-cross of creeks and valleys, all heavily forested, around the headwaters of the Trunkey Creek and the Abercrombie River. This wild and remote area was around 60 kilometres to the south of Bathurst and contained many places to shelter and to hide, including the complex that made up the Abercrombie Caves.

At the edge of this wilderness was a property named Mulgunnia, one of several properties in the Bathurst district owned by a pastoralist named Thomas Arkell. Behind the property was a feature known as

Arkell's Ridge and to the south beyond that feature was largely unexplored territory in 1830. Also beyond that ridge was Grove Creek, and if an explorer had pushed up Grove Creek at that time, he would soon have found the Abercrombie Archway and caves, as well as the spectacular 70-metre-high Grove Creek Falls, naturally occurring features destined to become popular attractions in years to come. Bypassing these, and pushing further into the wilderness, the explorer would have found a rocky glen, almost a valley leading off to one side.

It seems probable that Entwistle and his men used the Abercrombie Caves for shelter, and they certainly used the feature known as Stable Arch to stable their horses. Entwistle was too smart a person to establish a permanent base in the caves, though, because if he and his men were trapped inside, their options would be reduced to starve or surrender. Their camp near Grove Creek was far better; while the sides of the glen were steep, they were not insurmountable, but it would take an army to flush them out.

On the last weekend in September 1830, it was their base. From it, they were able to raid Mulgunnia and from there, they could ride quite easily to Thomas Arkell's home station, Charlton, located 20 kilometres to the north-east on the Campbell's River. Both properties yielded horses, arms and supplies and, satisfied with their work, Entwistle led his men back to camp sometime during the afternoon of Monday 27 September.

By that time, it had become obvious to all in and around Bathurst that something more than the irritation of a few absconders or an occasional bushranger was afoot. It was equally obvious that the limited police and military resources then in Bathurst might not be sufficient to protect the settlement and its inhabitants should Entwistle and his gang descend on the town. Reinforcements were on the way, and no-one doubted that weight of numbers would eventually lead to the destruction of the gang. Equally, no-one knew when that would be though, and in the meantime, the good people of Bathurst would need to look to their own resources for protection.

It was with this in mind that Major Macpherson called for a public meeting to be convened at the Bathurst Courthouse in the middle hours of the day on that Monday. It was a call supported by all the legal and administrative officers of the district, the magistrates, the Coroner, the manager of the Government Farm and the like. No records of proceedings or minutes were kept, but it is probable that at least 30 or more male residents attended.

After the usual debate and strong expressions of many emotions, the meeting resolved to do something positive. If enough of those present were prepared to volunteer their services, they would form a paramilitary unit to protect Bathurst and its surrounds from further depredations. At someone's suggestion — and Donald Macpherson is the most likely fit here — they would be constituted as a "corps of volunteer cavalry." Macpherson was again clearly identified as the instigator, appointing William Suttor as the unit's commander with his younger brother Charles as his deputy. Suttor said he would proudly accept the honour but would be equally happy to serve under another man should that man have stronger claims to leadership. No-one else stepped forward.

Suttor directed the other volunteers to return to their homes, if appropriate, to collect whatever arms, ammunition, supplies and horses they thought appropriate for the task, and to return to the courthouse no later than 5 p.m. that afternoon. Twelve men would assemble there at the hour specified, but they would not be the same twelve who had volunteered earlier in the day. Some had found that other matters were now more pressing, and so sent one of their men in their stead. It is also interesting to note that the volunteer unit was designated as a cavalry unit. Traditionally, cavalry were the eyes and ears for the larger infantry units.

Their role was to scout the enemy and to remain certain at all times of the enemy's strength and location so that the infantry could then bring them to a decisive battle. It is not certain whether or not William Suttor was aware of this.

*   *   *

The volunteers reassembled outside the courthouse at five 5 p.m., dressed for action and armed with an assortment of muskets, shotguns and pistols. There had been no real discussion about where Suttor's group would begin their search for Entwistle and his gang, and the need for such a discussion was removed by the arrival of a weary horse and rider. The rider said that he had come as fast as his horse would carry him from Charlton, Thomas Arkell's property on the Campbell's River, some 60 kilometres to the south. Entwistle and his gang had raided the farm earlier in the day and had stolen anything they thought might have been either useful or valuable. He had waited until they had left, the rider said, and had then taken one of the horses they had missed to bring the news to Bathurst as soon as possible.

William Suttor explained all this to his men and said that the troop would ride through the night to Charlton, seek the latest intelligence there and base their search on what they learned. The men then rode off into the gathering dusk, riding through the night at a reasonable pace and without taking unnecessary risks, before arriving at Arkell's station on Campbell's River shortly before dawn. As they all expected, Entwistle and his men were long gone, and had not been seen since departing with their loot eighteen hours earlier. Thomas Arkell himself was at Charlton, and after organising breakfast for Suttor's troop, told Suttor that he and his overseer, a Ticket of Leave man named Yates, would go with him as they were both familiar with the surrounding countryside.

As luck would have it, among the Aboriginals who were at Arkell's station seeking work were two who had previously worked for the Suttors and who William Suttor knew quite well. Their names were Moola and Woolloomooloo, and they agreed to work for Suttor to track down Entwistle and his men. It was late morning before men and horses were rested enough to continue. Moola and Woolloomooloo picked up the tracks left by the bushrangers quite easily, and the settler's party headed off in a general south-westerly direction. They skirted the Mulgunnia station and plunged into the heavy bushland beyond. The trail took them past the Warragamba River, the Abercrombie River and the nearby caves, and along the watercourse that Arkell said was Grove Creek. At the midpoint of the afternoon, Moola and Woolloomooloo slowed, and then stopped, telling Suttor that the bushrangers were now just a short distance ahead.

William Suttor called his troop to a halt immediately and directed that they all dismount. He asked Arkell and Yates to go forward with the trackers, ascertain the location and strength of the bushrangers' camp and then come straight back to where he and the others would be waiting with the horses. The four men were gone for less than half an hour, and when they returned, they said that Entwistle and his gang were camped in a rocky glen off the main valley they were following. It appeared to be quite a large encampment, but the nature of the terrain and the foliage in the glen made it difficult to estimate how many men were camped there. Entwistle did not seem to have posted any sentries or lookouts.

Suttor called all his men together and outlined the situation as he saw it. After detailing the bushrangers' campsite, its distance and apparent composition, he said that he estimated that there was around an hour's sunlight left, and then canvassed his men's opinions. One man suggested that they remain where they were for the time being. The best time to mount an attack against the camp, he reckoned, would be at either of two times. The first was when the bushrangers were eating dinner and would therefore be distracted. The second was around 3 a.m. in the morning when most, if not all, would be asleep.

Those who spoke up did so in favour of an immediate attack, and Suttor said that he, too, was of a like mind. They would attack as soon as possible and hopefully finish off the bushrangers before dark. The Aboriginals and a young man who had recently joined their party were directed to take the horses into the cover of some nearby trees and remain there until Suttor and the men returned. He then had his men check their arms and ammunition, before leading them silently up the valley and towards the glen.

*   *   *

As the scouts had reported, the bushrangers' camp was a short distance ahead. It was located in a side valley a bit larger than Suttor had anticipated, the valley's floor covered with small and large rocks, with the camp backing onto a fairly solid covering of bush. Although the men could not see what, if anything was hidden by those trees, Suttor suspected it might be the bushrangers' horses plus any supplies they wanted to keep under cover. There did not appear to be any high ground beyond the trees and towards the end of the little valley, which seemed to be open at both ends. The slopes on either side were quite steep and rocky, but also had a good covering of trees and shrubs. It was difficult to tell how many men there might be in the camp; several could be seen moving in and around the trees and rocks, and Suttor suspected that there were probably others either sitting or lying down, out of sight, as well.

Suttor made his plans quickly. He called the men together and outlined what he proposed to do. Four men would be sent to the rear of the little valley, using the natural cover along the valley's sides to move the four hundred or so metres to a position where they and their guns controlled any movement out of the valley at that end. The remainder of the force, ten men, would wait a few minutes to allow the blocking party to get into position and would then attack the bushrangers' camp from the front, making as much noise as possible. The hope was that the bushrangers would panic and attempt to flee. When they realised they were trapped, Suttor expected that they would all surrender.

The four men selected to be the ambush party checked their weapons carefully and then moved off on their mission. From where William Suttor stood, the men were visible as they moved carefully from cover to cover along the valley wall, however Suttor doubted that anyone in the valley below even knew they were there, such was the cover available to them. Suttor continued to watch the four until, when they were about a third of the way along the route they were following, one of the men tripped. As he struggled to retain his footing, one of his flailing legs dislodged quite a large rock which bounded and crashed its way through shrubs and bushes to the valley floor below. There was a moment of silence, then one of the bushrangers called out something which sounded like an extremely loud, "Hello!"

There was another moment of silence before all hell broke loose. Bushrangers jumped up from behind rocks and trees, grabbing weapons and calling out to one another, asking what was happening and what they should do. Most were looking up towards the slope where the rock had been dislodged. Taking advantage of the distraction, Arkell and Yates rose from where they had been crouching near Suttor, and ran towards the bushrangers' camp, shouting at the top of their voices and waving their muskets. This new source of danger seemed to discomfit the bushrangers, who fell back towards the trees at the rear of the camp. One or two of them fired in the general direction of the attackers, but their aim was hurried, and their shots had no effect.

Suttor and the others remained where they were, preparing to open fire on the bushrangers. During a hiatus that lasted only a few moments, several things happened. One was that Ralph Entwistle took charge of the bushrangers. Some in Suttor's party may have known him personally, while others may have recognised him by his size and colouring, but all soon understood who the bushrangers' leader was. He appeared from behind a tree where he had taken cover and immediately began to issue orders in a loud voice. Wearing a hat from which dozens of white ribbons swished and swayed, he directed his men to flush out Arkell and Yates, who were now in the rocks at the front of the camp.

Arkell and Yates now realised just how precarious their position was. They could clearly hear Entwistle directing his men to flank them, to move from cover to cover along the valley margins until they could clearly see the two men, take careful aim, and kill them both. Neither Arkell nor Yates was prepared to let this happen. Crouching low, and running as hard as they could, they made it back safely to where Suttor and his men remained ensconced among the trees and rocks of their own little fortress. A few seconds later, they were joined by the four from the valley side.

It was always going to be a stalemate as the sides were so evenly matched. For an hour, shots were exchanged along with a number of threats and general abuse. William Suttor and his men occupied what turned out to be a strong defensive position and none among them was prepared to mount the kind of charge that Arkell and Yates had tried at the beginning of the engagement. Their return, with the four from the valley's slopes meant that both sides had roughly the same number of men and weaponry, and both occupied positions which would be difficult for the other to overrun.

Things were a bit different, though, on the bushranger's side, where Entwistle could not be certain of either how many men he was facing or whether they were the advance unit of a much larger force or simply a civilian posse who had by chance stumbled across the bushrangers' hide-out. He chose to expose himself to the enemy, to gauge their numbers and their intentions, and to also embolden his own men. He stepped out from behind a protecting tree on several occasions, drawing fire each time; it was said later that the tree had been struck by 15 musket balls. It was risky behaviour, but it did give him a good idea of where Suttor's men were and how many of them he was facing.

Entwistle slowly got the better of Suttor by constantly calling out to his men, telling them to maintain cover and, where possible, to carefully move forward to the flanks of Suttor's position, always noting where the others were from their gun flashes and the gun smoke from their muskets. When they chose to fire, he told them, they should choose their targets and remain as still as possible when they fired. "Do not waste your ammunition, boys," he shouted. "Choose your targets and make every ball count."

Entwistle was determined to take the battle to Suttor. He abandoned his position among the trees to take cover among the rocks and boulders strewn across the valley floor. At one point, he jumped up onto a rock, the better to direct his men's fire. He instantly attracted fire himself, and one musket ball was seen to clip a lock of hair off close to his ear. But his men continued to seek ways to move forward. Two of them were hit and wounded as they did so, but Entwistle simply called out to them to make their way to the rear for treatment. William Suttor was not alone in thinking that Entwistle had been involved in this kind of fighting before.

After almost an hour of exchanging shots it was beginning to grow dark in the mountains, and Suttor was now faced with two problems. The first was that his party was almost out of ammunition. Suttor himself had carried 12 cartridges and the last of these had been fired some time earlier. He guessed that both sides had fired around 300 shots between them and, while he had no idea about Entwistle's supply of ammunition, he was very well aware of his own; all his men were telling him that they were down to their last one or two cartridges. The second problem was related to the first. The bushrangers were, slowly but inexorably, moving closer to his position. If they realised that the lack of fire from the posse was due to a lack of ammunition rather than a lack of targets, they would rush his position and it would be all over very quickly.

It was a delicate situation, but one that Suttor thought could best be met with a bold manoeuvre. Crawling from cover to cover, he told his men that the best way to save themselves was to tackle the situation head-on. They would charge the bushrangers, he said, but their charge would be over in just a few yards. Suttor and his men would scream, and they would fire their guns and, in the confusion that was sure to follow, they would retreat rapidly to where their horses were being held. They would then ride back to Charlton, notify the authorities of what had happened, and then plan their next move.

When all were ready, Suttor jumped up and yelled out at the top of his voice to charge the bushrangers, to finish off every last one of them. As he did so, his dozen men all jumped up and ran forward with him, with several firing their guns in the general direction of the bushrangers. The ruse had some immediate success; five bushrangers appeared from their various hiding places and started to run towards the trees at the rear of the campsite. Suttor himself was lucky to survive the ruse. When he jumped up from cover, several bushrangers fired at him. One of their musket balls clipped his beard while another passed straight through his hat without touching his head.

Suttor's plan was almost completely successful. When he and his men stopped in their tracks after their short charge towards the bushrangers there was obvious confusion ahead of them. As quickly as they had run forward, they now started to make a measured retreat. They fell back in stages and in groups, with some always facing backwards and others firing an occasional shot at the bushrangers who pursued them.

If Entwistle had been fooled by the tactic, it did not take him long to recover. Realising that the posse which had come after them was now retreating, he rallied his men and called them forward. He again climbed onto a rock to direct his men, calling out a running commentary as he did so, directing his men to the flanks rather than directly at Suttor and his men, and directing their fire at individual targets that he selected. In doing so, he revealed that he had mistakenly identified William Suttor as Thomas Evernden. Every time he glimpsed Suttor, he would call out, "Evernden's with them. Kill him! Don't worry about the others. Kill Evernden!" In the stillness around dusk, his calls rang out across the valley.

Among the imprecations he hurled at Suttor/Evernden were also a number of clear and calculated directions to his men to aim carefully and not waste their ammunition, to use the cover of the trees and the rocks, and to try to catch Suttor/Evernden and his men in a crossfire. He was no fool, either. The light was now fading fast and it seemed to him that the leader of the posse was withdrawing his men to a grove of trees. Entwistle did not know what was in that grove but, on one look, he might be in the process of leading his own men into some kind of ambush. It was not a chance he was prepared to take. With calls, signs and whistles, he directed the bushrangers back to the campsite they would soon abandon. They might lose a campsite, but they would live to fight another day.

*   *   *

Charles Suttor would be the last to leave what his brother would later call "the battlefield", somewhere in the rugged country where Grove Creek rises. When he was certain that Entwistle and his gang were no longer in pursuit he, too, mounted his horse and rode hard to catch up with the others.

Moola and Woolloomooloo and the young European had been waiting with the horses at the designated spot, and when Suttor and his men arrived there, they all quietly climbed up into their saddles. Suttor had probably intended to ride all the way back to Campbell's River and Arkell's head station there, but the weather turned foul, heavy rain sweeping across the ranges. Rather than risk losing their way or plunging into one of the many gullies that criss-crossed their route, Suttor called a halt in the first relatively flat and sheltered spot they found. They had ridden for more than an hour, and Suttor correctly guessed that the bushrangers had no intention of following them. However, the weather also meant that it was not possible to light a campfire, so Suttor and his men spent an uncomfortable night with the storm crashing around them. Their mood did not improve in the morning when daylight revealed that half the horses had wandered away in the darkness.

Their departure the next day — by now it was Wednesday 29 September — was therefore delayed until all the missing horses had been recovered. It was around the middle of the day before they came down out of the hills to the flatter land below Mulgunnia and the road that would take them all the way to Charlton. They had not travelled far down that road when they met another party of horsemen, the detachment of mounted police under the command of James Brown. Suttor and Brown exchanged both pleasantries and intelligence. Suttor was able to give Brown a detailed description of the bushrangers' campsite and an estimate of their numbers and weaponry. He declined Brown's invitation to join forces, citing the condition of his men and his horses and the fact that they were all out of ammunition.

Suttor and his party arrived at Charlton late in the day, and he immediately began a letter to Donald Macpherson in Bathurst, providing what he considered an accurate account of what had occurred when his party clashed with Entwistle's bushrangers at Grove Creek. He gave as much detail as he thought appropriate and made special mention of the "profusion" of white ribbons worn by Entwistle and the fact that other members of the gang had also attached white ribbons to their headwear as well. Suttor's letter suggested that he had done the best that could be expected, and that he would now wait for further directions from Macpherson.

Another letter was also drafted at Charlton that evening. Not all his party were happy with how the various situations they confronted had been handled by William Suttor. One of them wrote a letter of criticism to several Sydney newspapers. The correspondent used the pseudonym, "Eyewitness", and was probably Thomas Arkell himself. The writer's criticism boiled down to three main points. The first was that it was foolish to attack at the time they did, when all the bushrangers were both awake and alert. It would have been far better to have taken the bushrangers unaware, in the small hours of the morning, perhaps, or when they were preparing and consuming their evening meal.

The second criticism was that when the first attack was mounted, it was not pressed home with any vigour. When the call was given, only a few rushed forwards; the rest were prepared to sit in cover, taking an occasional pot shot at a distant and fleeting target. Finally, Suttor held his men in position for too long. They were almost entirely out of ammunition when Suttor finally gave the order to withdraw. It was good luck rather than good leadership that allowed them to escape without any casualties.

William Suttor and Eyewitness were not the only two putting pen to paper on the subject of Ralph Entwistle and his direct challenge to authority. When Donald Macpherson received William Suttor's letter, he immediately moved to establish a second posse, another "corps of volunteer cavalry." He was obviously concerned about the leadership of these little units as he appointed a serving soldier, a Lieutenant Delaney, to command the unit. Another dozen volunteers offered themselves almost immediately, and Delaney led them straight out to search for the bushrangers.

It was at this point that the colony at large began to learn that something was amiss out on the western frontier, that something beyond the usual mischief caused by absconders was taking place out there. There was some speculation about what may have caused the uprising — if that was what had actually taken place — and there was further speculation about the actual dimensions of that uprising. There was talk in the newspapers, and in the taverns as well, of a general rising of convicts beyond the Blue Mountains, centred on a place called "Mudgee", one that was linked to possible uprisings elsewhere. It was also rumoured that Governor Darling was about to request that a special "Bushrangers Act" be passed to suppress the lawlessness he believed was now rampant throughout the colony.

In his report, William Suttor would write, "What the object of the men is who have disturbed the country is to me a mystery, but it appears they have long been planning the 'turn-out', as they call it." His father, George Suttor, also took to writing letters to the press and to the authorities as well. In somewhat purple prose, George Suttor would describe Entwistle and his band as, "the most formidable, desperate set of ruffians that ever infested the country". Like many others, William and George Suttor had learned that Ralph Entwistle and the band he led were without fear of consequences, well-organised and well supplied with arms, ammunition and horses.

They were about to learn that things could, indeed, get worse.

To the Lachlan

Had William Suttor and his men agreed to Lieutenant James Brown's suggestion that they joined forces, Ralph Entwistle's little rebellion may well have been over the next day. Suttor had with him the two trackers, Moola and Woolloomooloo, who would have been as effective as scouts as they had been as trackers. There would also have been a body of men with firsthand experience of how Entwistle and his bushrangers actually fought: their tactics, which suggested some familiarity with the theory of infantry skirmishing; their firing discipline; and, most of all, the fact that Ralph Entwistle was a leader who was both personally brave and tactically astute.

After they parted, Brown led his men off into the bush to find the site of the clash between bushrangers and posse, which he would use as a starting point in his search for the gang. Suttor rode away to Thomas Arkell's station where he would compose a letter; a report on the clash which, really, seems to have been written with at least one eye on history. He would play no further part in the events which unfolded.

*   *   *

Scattered throughout the Central West of New South Wales are a number of topographical features with names such as "Bushranger's Hill", "Bald

Ridge" and "One Tree Hill". Features with those or similar names weave in and out of Entwistle's narrative from this point forward, but they are usually mentioned in isolation and in a manner which implies that everyone will be familiar with those specific locations. This is simply not the case; names, description and usage change over time, and what everyone understood as "Bushranger's Hill" almost 200 years ago is not necessarily the case today. However, while the locations may be something of a mystery, the sequence of events is not.

Ralph Entwistle guessed correctly that there would be a follow-up to the attack launched on his campsite by the Suttor party. While that party had been repulsed, it was a close-run affair and it may have had a different outcome had not one of Suttor's men dislodged a rock as he attempted to set up a blocking party at the rear of the campsite. Entwistle may have remained with his men at that spot overnight and, if he did so, he would certainly have organised a system of sentries. The next day, Thursday 30 September, Entwistle led his men away from the camp near Grove Creek. Any movement to the east or north-east would have taken him towards the areas that he and his men had already raided, so this time he moved in a generally westerly direction.

Entwistle also posted lookouts ahead and behind the main group. Sometime during the day, probably early in the afternoon, the rear guard reported that they were being followed by a small troop of mounted police. Entwistle decided to ambush that troop because his own band clearly outnumbered them. He rode ahead, searching for a suitable ambush site, and soon found one. It was again a glen, or a small valley, with good cover on either side where the relatively gentle slopes had many vantage points screened by rocks and trees. It was a position that would later be described as almost impregnable.

Lieutenant James Brown and his men really did not know what hit them. They had been following a faint trail that wound through the bush, sometimes a bit up and down, but generally following a level gradient. Again, the troopers were sometimes hemmed in by trees, riding astride their horses in single file; at other places, there was a light cover of trees and their way passed through almost meadow-like conditions where two or more could ride abreast. They had just entered such an area when all hell broke loose. Gunshots and abuse rained down upon them from both sides. Horses screamed and reared in pain and fright, troopers called out for help, for their mothers, for something to take the pain away.

Above it all, the troopers heard James Brown calling out for them to fall back, and those who were capable of doing so did just that. Some were wounded and all were demoralised. Brown had no doubts whatsoever about who was responsible, and he was able to bring some order to the situation, some calm to his men, by directing them to take up firing positions, check themselves for wounds and then check their arms and accoutrements. All firing by the bushrangers had now ceased, but Brown did nothing beyond urging his men to remain calm and vigilant.

Minute succeeded minute, and there was still no movement, let alone gunfire, from the little valley where the ambush had taken place. Brown was the only officer present, and he took that responsibility seriously. He would not send anyone to do something that he was not prepared to do himself, so he carefully went forward, moving from cover to cover until he was in the middle of what had been a battle ground 20 minutes earlier. He moved up the nearest slope, expecting a shot to ring out at any moment. There were no bushrangers there, although he could clearly see where several had taken up firing positions.

Brown returned to the valley floor and signalled to his men to come forward. A search of the area revealed the extent to which the mounted police had been caught completely unawares. Two troopers lay dead on the ground, several others had sustained bullet wounds of varying seriousness and there were five horses that were either dead or so badly wounded that they would be shot to put them out of their misery. It was a long way back to civilization, but James Brown would walk all the way. Some of his troopers would double up on the remaining horses, but Brown would not be one of them. His own horse was uninjured, but he would walk and lead it by its reins; bound tightly across its back were the bodies of his two dead troopers. He looked back one more time and saw there were no trees on the skyline of one of the ridges that flanked the little valley. In his report, he would name it Bald Ridge.

*   *   *

In the midst of the hysteria generated in some quarters by the early reports coming from Bathurst, there was a report in one of the Sydney newspapers, *The Australian*, which attempted to provide some context for those reports.

> *A strong body of the military was suddenly marched off from town on Sunday last, in the direction of Bathurst with orders to act against the   prisoners who are reported to have risen between that settlement and Wellington Valley, and to be in some force under the direction of an individual who formerly held a commission in the army.*
>
> *The reports are various and conflicting.*
>
> *Some represent the Moreton Bay prisoners as having risen in a body, overcome the guard, and marched across the road by which a number of government cattle were lately driven to Wellington Valley. Other reports state that the insurgents are confined principally to that part of the country and the vicinity of Bathurst, where several of both sides are said to have fallen.*
>
> *We can as yet arrive at no authentic conclusions on this subject. As usual, many circumstances trivial in themselves are exaggerated*

as great important events. It seems pretty clear however, that some
disturbance of a more than ordinarily exciting character has taken
place. It is what we have long since foreseen. Severity, as a rule, defeats
its own end.

No doubt an ill-organised, undisciplined body of prisoners may be
put down by force of arms; but it is always better to avoid coming to
such circumstances. Were the prisoners in iron and road gangs better
fed and better worked, and more judicious incitements held out to
them to reform, much benefit, we are persuaded, would accrue to all
parties concerned.

The Australian was a small newspaper, however there would have
been some support for what were liberal views on crime and punishment for the time and place. But New South Wales remained primarily
a penal colony, and one where — despite the growing number of free
settlers and emancipated convicts — the authority of the state relied
on convicts remaining convicts until the state itself decided they were
free. Absconding was one thing, becoming bushrangers was another.
Defeating a body of mounted police put a larger and more threatening
veneer over both. It was now, literally, a struggle to the death.

*   *   *

A pattern now began to emerge in the movements of Ralph Entwistle
and his gang of bushrangers. Apparently realising that the areas directly
south and south-west of Bathurst that had become their home range were
now too dangerous because of the various police parties and settlers'
posse's that seemed to be combing that area for them, Entwistle continued to lead his men in a general westerly direction. Their path followed
the course of the Abercrombie River and then the Lachlan River after

the Abercrombie flowed into it. They kept away from the farms and roads along the valley floors and seemed to have raided only one or two farms as they travelled, again in a possible effort to throw the police off their trail.

By 1830, the frontier lay beyond the Lachlan, and it appears that Ralph Entwistle was attempting to lead his men over that frontier and out of the reach of the law. Like all the rivers on that side of the mountains, the Lachlan flowed in a general south-westerly direction. Many in the colony believed that all those rivers flowed into a vast inland sea. If that were true, it would have been possible to live a reasonable life well beyond the limits of settlement. If this was the escape that Entwistle was now seeking for himself and his followers — and the direction he took suggests that it was — he and those men were now in a race to see whether they could find a sanctuary in the great unknown before the forces they knew were behind them finally caught up.

*   *   *

Those forces were now considerable. Lieutenant Delaney and his civilian volunteer cavalry were out and about, sweeping through the bushland to the south-west of Bathurst, while Lieutenant James Brown had reformed his troop of mounted police and was again patrolling in the region where he and his men had been ambushed. Another patrol of mounted police led by a Lieutenant Moore even had some success in the pursuit. Moore's patrol found one of the absconders who was able to convince them that he was actually making his way to the farm from which he had absconded. To guarantee his bona fides, he volunteered to lead Moore to the cache of arms and ammunition he had been guarding for Ralph Entwistle. He led the patrol straight to it, and the weaponry was recovered and taken back to Bathurst. Even William Suttor volunteered to take another party out.

However, almost all of those who were out searching for the bushrangers concentrated their efforts in areas which had already been searched, hoping that Entwistle and his men had chosen to remain in the district that they knew best. Because all the civilians and most of the police were also from the areas immediately around Bathurst, they were unwilling to leave their settlement and their farms exposed, even when Entwistle was reported raiding properties much further to the west. The general attitude was that, after what had happened to Suttor's party and Brown's mounted police, it might be best that nothing more be attempted until further reinforcements arrived from Sydney. This meant that Lachlan Macalister's mounted police from Goulburn and Horatio Walpole's regular soldiers from Sydney would have to catch the gang.

The more mobile of these two was Macalister's troopers, who were also fortunate to have Lachlan Macalister as their leader. Macalister had been born on the Isle of Skye in 1797. In 1815, he had purchased a commission in the 48th Regiment of Foot and was despatched to New South Wales with his regiment two years later. After a year on garrison duty in Sydney, Macalister's regiment was sent to Port Dalrymple on the Tamar River in northern Van Diemen's Land. When the 48th was recalled to England, Macalister opted to remain in New South Wales and in 1820 was living in Newcastle. There, he became friendly with two of John Macarthur's sons, and in 1824 he was granted land alongside their properties at Taralga in the Southern Highlands. Macalister bought breeding stock, both cattle and sheep, from the Macarthurs and established a fine pastoral run at Taralga.

In 1826, Macalister was appointed as a magistrate to sit at Goulburn, and in 1827 he was made both Resident Magistrate and Officer in Charge of the mounted police at Goulburn. It was a timely appointment for at that time absconders and bushrangers were becoming a significant problem in the Southern Highlands. Most dangerous of them all was the gang led by John Donohoe, now operating in the area. It was Lachlan Macalister's troopers, with Macalister leading them, which staged the ambush near Bringelly which killed Donohoe and broke up his gang. Macalister was wounded, though not seriously, in that clash.

He was again in action when news of the Entwistle outbreak, along with a request for assistance, reached Goulburn. By the time he arrived in the Bathurst area, the main actions had all taken place and the bush-rangers were making their way to the west; Macalister led his men after them. A number of farms reported seeing Entwistle's gang, some others were held up, and by the second week of October, Macalister was certain that he was very close to his quarry. On 13 October, Entwistle and his men swept down on George Ranken's Lachlan River property, Bula Jackey, south of Limestone Creek and not far from where the current city of Forbes stands. The gang were riding away carelessly, and without a seeming worry in the world, when they literally rode into Lachlan Macalister and his troopers.

It was a short, sharp and confused affair, a melee of men wheeling on horses, firing, and then looking for somewhere safe to retire to and there reload before re-joining the fray. Macalister himself was one of the first casualties; spotting the officer, Ralph Entwistle took aim with his pistol and fired. The ball smashed into Macalister's left forearm, breaking the bone, but not unhorsing him.

"That's number one, boys," Entwistle called out. *"Take 'em steady."*

Although quite badly wounded and in a lot of pain, Macalister remained in the fight. He drew his own pistol and, holding it across his broken arm, took careful aim at Ralph Entwistle and fired. The ball ploughed through the bushranger's side, a painful wound but not one that would be fatal. As Entwistle swivelled and looked for some shelter, Macalister called out at the top of his voice, *"And that makes number two."*

The clash was over as quickly as it had begun. Seeing Entwistle wounded and seemingly retreating, the other bushrangers also turned and rode away, clustered around their wounded leader. It was not a rout, but it was clearly a defeat, made doubly bitter by Entwistle's wound. It showed that he, too, was human and not the invulnerable leader that some had come to believe he was. One or two of the other bushrangers had also been wounded in the exchange. None were serious but all would need some kind of treatment. Entwistle led them away, towards the west of course, until they came to a small hillock. It had rocks and a few trees for cover and, while not impregnable, would hold off a troop of mounted police until nightfall made an escape possible.

Macalister made no attempt to follow the bushrangers but sent two troopers to trail them at a distance, see where they went, and then report back. A couple of his troopers had also received slight wounds in the encounter with Entwistle, and Macalister knew his own wound would need to be cleaned and his broken arm placed in a splint. Like Entwistle, he led his men back to a safe spot where they could camp overnight, and he could allocate duties to his men. One of these was to take a brief report he would write back to Bathurst and bring other troopers and soldiers back to where had made this campsite. Later, that messenger returned not half an hour after he had ridden away. He reported that a company of soldiers were on their way as he spoke and would arrive within the hour.

*   *   *

Captain Horatio Walpole took his duty seriously. When ordered to march a company of soldiers to Bathurst — and beyond if necessary — to bring a gang of bushrangers to justice, he made the necessary plans, issued the necessary orders and led his men out of their Sydney barracks on Sunday 26 September. Two and a half weeks' later, he led them to the camp they would share with Lachlan Macalister's mounted police for the night which was either 13 or 14 October. It would never be remembered as one of the British Army's great marches, but it was an outstanding feat, nevertheless.

Walpole and his men marched out along what was now a well-travelled road, past Penrith and along Cox's Line of Road. They marched at a steady pace, with regular halts and with overnight bivouacs in tents at the end of each day. When they eventually marched into Bathurst after almost two weeks on the road, most assumed they would now be based at the army barracks located there. They were wrong, with Walpole marching his men out onto the plains beyond. Now they had an actual objective, though, as mounted police had brought them regular updates on the suspected whereabouts of Entwistle and his gang. After a final forced march through unexplored bush, Walpole led his men into Lachlan Macalister's camp late on the afternoon of 13 October.

Walpole and Macalister discussed their options. Macalister's mounted troopers reported that Entwistle and his men had occupied a strong position on a rocky knoll a short distance to the west and appeared to have reinforced it. The officer decided to reconnoitre that position at first light the following morning, and then formulate their plans on the basis of what they found there.

A small group of mounted police rode out before dawn the next morning. Walpole rode out with them and made a careful reconnaissance of the area in which Entwistle and his men were encamped. Satisfied with what he saw and realising just how few men Entwistle had with him, Walpole suggested an immediate attack, a decision with which Macalister concurred. A trooper was sent back to urge the soldiers, who had marched out at dawn, to hurry forward.

In Ralph Entwistle's camp, things were already depressed that morning. The wound Entwistle had suffered at Macalister's hand the previous day was little more than an inconvenience to him but was viewed as an ill-starred omen by some of his men who had previously believed Entwistle to be invulnerable. Two others in his band had also been wounded in the clash with the mounted police while, overnight, three others had left the campsite, with or without Entwistle's permission. Although they shouldn't have been surprised, it seems that they were when, shortly after dawn the next morning, an army officer on horseback called upon them to surrender. Behind him, two lines of infantry were drawn up, muskets at the ready. They were flanked on both sides by armed men on horseback, a mixture of soldiers and mounted police.

When there was no response to a second call to surrender, the officer rode back to where a small cluster of other horsemen sat behind the centre of the infantry line. That officer then shouted out the order for rapid fire. The first rank of soldiers lifted their muskets and fired, then knelt down to reload. As they were doing so, the second line stepped forward, shouldered their muskets, fired, then stepped back and knelt to reload, as the first rank rose, aimed and fired again.

In their little campsite cum stronghold, Ralph Entwistle and his men tried to burrow in behind any cover they could find. There was an almost continuous roar of musketry from the double line of infantry, and the heavy musket balls they fired thudded into both earth and trees or ricocheted, screaming, off the small and large boulders scattered throughout the area. Exposure to the fire would bring about certain death while any attempt to escape would be cut off by the mounted troopers who sat patiently astride their horses just waiting for an opportunity to do just that. During the brief intervals between the volleys, Entwistle's men called out to him in fear.

"Let us surrender," they called out, "let us surrender before we are all killed in this Godforsaken place."

During another brief pause in the firing, Entwistle waved his hat, with its white ribbons still attached, above the rock behind which he was still crouching. He heard a bugle call, followed by a shouted command to cease fire. That same voice called out to Entwistle and his men to lay down their weapons, stand with their hands in the air and walk to where a mixed group of soldiers and troopers awaited them. As they did so, a line of soldiers covered them with raised muskets. Several men were then despatched to search the bushrangers' campsite and the bush nearby. They were to return with the bushrangers' horses and weapons, and anything else they found there.

While they were doing just that, a second group of soldiers and police firstly searched the bushrangers and then fitted both manacles and leg irons to them all, Entwistle and the other two wounded included. The various groups were then called together and formed into a column. Headed by Horatio Walpole and Lachlan Macalister, it contained the line of shackled prisoners with mounted police on either side, two lines of soldiers walking abreast following. At Walpole's shouted command, they moved off towards Bathurst; it was no longer a forced march, and Macalister estimated that it would take them two days, or three at most. Not that it really mattered now. For the prisoners, time was coming to an end; for all the others, it was just the beginning of the rest of their lives.

THE RECKONING

On 20 October 1830, the secretary to Governor Ralph Darling issued General Order No. 15. The Order opened with the statement that, *"His Excellency the Governor has much satisfaction in announcing the capture of the whole of the insurgents.... who lately infested the neighbourhood of Bathurst, and committed a series of the most wanton outrages in that district."*

The Order went on to personally identify and congratulate those the Governor considered most responsible for bringing Ralph Entwistle's Ribbon Gang to justice: Major Donald Macpherson, Captain Horatio Walpole, and Lieutenants James Brown and Lachlan Macalister. In the order, Darling then announced an increase in the mounted police establishment before closing with a warning to settlers against allowing their government men to possess weapons.

Capturing the gang was one thing but bringing them to trial proved to be something else again. In New South Wales at that time, there was a general and officially approved expectation that prisoners charged with serious crimes should be tried in the district in which the crimes had been committed. As the New South Wales Supreme Court had not sat in judgement anywhere outside Sydney up to that point, a Special Commission had to be issued authorising the court to sit at Bathurst. This was completed at Governor Darling's direction, and on 21 October the *Sydney Gazette* published the necessary proclamation. That proclamation allowed the Supreme Court of New South Wales to sit in hearings at Bathurst and directed the court's Chief Justice, Sir Francis Forbes, to adjudicate at the sitting. The trial of Entwistle and his gang was to be conducted at the Bathurst Courthouse and was to commence on 30 October. Forbes departed for Bathurst the next day, escorted by two mounted policemen.

The men who were to be tried before this special sitting of the Supreme Court were already awaiting Sir Francis in Bathurst. Ralph Entwistle and nine companions had been marched across the plains and foothills to Bathurst and were now housed, and closely guarded, in the settlement's primitive gaol. Neither Entwistle nor his fellow bushrangers were particularly communicative; the most Entwistle would offer up was that his gang had consisted of just 15 men for most of its history. Of those, two had died of wounds they had suffered in the various clashes with police and settlers, while three had either left or been sent away the evening before the gang surrendered to Walpole and Macalister's combined force. Mostly, though, Entwistle and the others kept very much to themselves.

Forbes convened his court briefly on 29 October. A jury of army officers was empanelled, and the various court officials reminded of what was both required and expected. The court was then adjourned until the following morning.

*   *   *

One of the first orders of business when the court reconvened the following morning was the arraignment of the prisoners on the various charges that had been brought forward, all of which carried the death penalty. Ralph Entwistle, William Gahan, Michael Kearney, Patrick Gleeson, Thomas Dunne and John Shepherd were all charged in the murder of John, alias James Greenwood. The information offered to support the charge contained four counts. Entwistle, Gahan and Kearney were all charged with the wilful murder of Greenwood at Bartlett's on 23 September 1830 by shooting him with a loaded gun or pistol. Gleeson, Dunne and Shepherd were all charged with being present, and aiding and assisting in the commission of the crime. All six were committed to trial on those counts.

Dominick Daley, James Driver, John Kenny and Robert Webster were charged with stealing from the house of one John Brown at Dunn's Plain on 26 September 1830, and of putting the said John Brown in fear of his life. Those four were additionally charged with the commission of the same offences, on the same day, at the house of Samuel Sealy, also of Dunn's Plain. Entwistle, Gahan and Kearney were included in both charges but were not arraigned because they were already facing capital punishment on the murder charges. Daley, Driver, Kenny and Webster were all indicted on both charges, and the proceedings now moved forward to the trial stage.

*   *   *

In the case of the wilful murder of James Greenwood, evidence for the prosecution was offered by two assigned servants: a ticket of leave man who was now the overseer of Thomas Evernden's property, Bartlett's; and by Thomas Evernden himself. The three primary witnesses told the court a story that varied very little between the tellers. All described how a group of armed men had ridden up to the main buildings at the farm quite early one morning late in the September just passed. They testified that all the men who rode in were armed, some with muskets or shotguns, others with pistols and some with both.

When they learned that Thomas Evernden was not present at the property, the armed men insisted that all those who worked at the farm be assembled in front of the huts in which they lived. The assembled men were then told that they should join the armed men and ride away from the farm to freedom. James Greenwood had also left his hut, and the leader of the gang addressed him specifically, saying he **must** accompany them when they left.

James Greenwood simply refused to go away with the armed men, whose leader said it would be best for him if he did so because, if he didn't, they would simply shoot him where he stood. All three witnesses then described how Greenwood again refused to leave with the armed men and how he opened his shirt and, pointing to his breast, said that none of the men present were game enough to shoot him. As Greenwood glared at the armed men, two of them fired at him. The witnesses all identified Entwistle and William Gahan as the men who fired those shots.

All three then described how James Greenwood put both hands to his chest and called out, *"Oh, Lord,"* before staggering back towards the door into his cabin. He seemed to be disoriented, a little lost, as he tried to feel his way back into the cabin. He was using the door frame as a support when a third man they all identified as Michael Kearney, fired a third shot into Greenwood's back. After this, the three described how Greenwood then lowered himself to the floor in front of his fireplace and neither moved nor spoke again.

The evidence offered after this graphic description was almost anti-climactic. The Government Medical Officer testified that he had examined the body of James Greenwood and found two gunshot wounds in the chest, both close to the heart, and a third in Greenwood's back, concluding that Greenwood died as a direct result of those wounds. Thomas Evernden confirmed that the assigned servants and Ticket of Leave man all worked on his property, that Greenwood's hut had been ransacked and that he was subsequently able to identify that some of the clothing worn by the prisoners had previously been worn by James Greenwood. Both of Evernden's assigned servants had left with Entwistle, but both had also returned to Bartlett's when they were given the opportunity to do so by Entwistle, and Evernden confirmed both their absence and their return. Those two also confirmed the presence of all those in the dock at Greenwood's murder.

There was scarcely a break in the routine of the trial when the witnesses' presentations were completed. The prisoners were briefly removed from the courtroom, and when they were brought back a few minutes later, it was to learn that all those charged had been found guilty on all counts. After this, they were subjected to a little homily by Chief Justice Forbes on the folly of crime and on their hope for redemption in the next world, something they certainly hadn't found in this one. Forbes then sentenced them all to be hanged by the neck until dead, and set the execution date as Tuesday 2 November, three days hence.

After the prisoners had been led from the courtroom, Robert Webster, James Driver, Dominick Daley and John Kenny were brought in to replace them in the dock. The four were told that they were charged with stealing from the residence of John Brown at Dunn's Plain on 26 September. The theft involved various goods and was, moreover, committed in a manner which placed the aforesaid John Brown in bodily fear.

Evidence was then offered that the four prisoners, in the company of several others not in the dock, went to John Brown's farm on the day in question and asked for Brown's overseer to be brought to them. That overseer was not at the farm; Brown had sent him away as soon as he learned of Ralph Entwistle's rebellion as he knew there was bad blood between the overseer and several of the men who had joined Entwistle's band. While there appeared to be some disappointment at that news, it did not prevent the four accused from taking whatever they wanted before they departed. The witnesses then confirmed that no-one had been physically injured during the raid, although there was no doubt that there would have been had anyone on the farm offered any resistance. They also confirmed that, when the gang was captured, several of them were wearing articles that had been taken from Brown's farm. All four men in the dock were positively identified as being part of the gang that carried out the raid.

There was another brief interval as the prisoners were removed and the jury considered its verdict. After just a few minutes, the prisoners were led back into the courtroom to learn that they had been found guilty on all charges. Forbes spoke briefly about crime and punishment before sentencing Robert Webster, Dominick Daley, James Driver and John Kenny to die on the same gallows and on the same day as their friends had been sentenced to earlier.

*　　*　　*

All those present at the proceedings that day — court officials and witnesses alike — would later recall the grim determination with which the prisoners listened to their fate unfold. Neither Entwistle nor any other of those who appeared in the dock that day showed any regret for what they had done or fear of what they were about to face. They seemed to be the hardened men they had by now become and, when asked whether they had anything to say before sentence was passed, replied as if with one voice, saying they were quite ready to receive what they knew they were fated to receive.

*　　*　　*

Preparations for that fate had actually commenced before Sir Francis Forbes handed down any sentences. Again, standard procedure at the time required that condemned men be comforted and attended by clergymen of their own faith in the lead-up to their execution. Nine of the ten men sentenced to hang by Chief Justice Forbes were Roman Catholic and the nearest Catholic priest was then in Sydney. Had he waited until news of the conviction and sentences arrived in Sydney, he would not have had sufficient time to travel out to Bathurst before the sentences were carried out.

Fortunately, Father John Joseph Therry was no ordinary Catholic priest. He was one of just two Catholic clergymen appointed to New South Wales in 1820, with both Church and Colonial Office approval, and since his arrival in the colony had seemed determined to make up for the 30 plus years that the spiritual needs of Catholics in New South Wales had been ignored. Before the Ribbon Gang Trial had even commenced, Father Therry had written to Governor Darling, saying that he believed that at least some of what he termed "the infatuated insurgents" would be convicted of the crimes of which they had been accused and would subsequently be sentenced to death for committing. Therry then expressed his desire to minister to those men who might be comforted by his presence and asked that horses be provided at government stations between Sydney and Bathurst to facilitate his travel.

The day after Governor Darling received the letter from Therry, the Colonial Secretary wrote back to the priest. Therry was informed that the only place on the Bathurst Road where the government could supply a horse was at the station located at Emu Plains. The superintendent there had already been informed that he was to comply with Father Therry's requests. That was enough for the priest, who set off for Bathurst almost immediately. If he rode quickly enough, he figured he would have two full days to save the condemned men's souls.

There was just one Protestant among the bushrangers, James Driver, and his spiritual needs could be met by someone a lot closer to home, the Reverend John Espy Keane, the rector of the Anglican Holy Trinity Church at nearby Kelso. The experience of ministering to a condemned man may have been only marginally less traumatic for Keane than it was for those awaiting execution. During one of his visits to the gaol to see Driver, Ralph Entwistle sidled up alongside the Anglican priest and asked him if he would be accompanying the condemned men to the gallows. When Keane said that he intended to do just that, Entwistle smiled and said, *"Well, just don't get too close to me. I might just take it upon myself to grab you and take you with me to wherever it is I might be going."*

Keane would never be sure whether or not Entwistle was joking.

*   *   *

Prior to the trial and conviction of the members of what was now being referred to as "The Ribbon Gang", all capital trials for offences committed in the Bathurst district were transferred to Sydney, and any consequent executions were also carried out there. The establishment of a Special Commission to allow the trial to be held in Bathurst also allowed for any death sentences that were handed down to be also carried out there. The hangings ordered by Chief Justice Forbes, to be held in public, would be the first ever conducted in Bathurst and the authorities there were determined that nothing would go wrong.

A team of assigned servants was sent out to a hill near The Rocks on the Orange Road, and there cut down and trimmed trees before a team of carpenters directed the sawing of the trunks into beams, struts, uprights and planks which would be fashioned into the gallows from which ten men would be launched into eternity. For years afterwards, the hill from which that timber was taken would be known as "Gallows Hill." A site for the execution was also chosen. In 1830, Bathurst was still a frontier settlement, its public and private buildings constructed wherever space and gradient allowed their building rather than according to any pre-ordained plan. On an open space set in the middle of several of those buildings, the gallows were built, and built in a way which meant the viewing public would be downhill from the action.

Tuesday, 2 November 1830, was a beautiful late spring day in Bathurst. It had been mild overnight, and the day promised to be clear, so by the middle of the afternoon, it was likely to be very warm with a hint of the blazing summer to come. The little crowd that had gathered below the scaffold on the side of a small hill in the middle of the settlement were not there to discuss the weather; they were there to see the end of Ralph Entwistle and his by now-infamous gang of bushrangers. It was still quite early in the day when the gaol gates opened, and armed soldiers led out six men whose arms had been secured behind their backs with manacles. Entwistle himself was easily recognisable; he was a bit taller than the others and had distinctive, strawberry blonde hair. There was also something of an air about him, something that suggested he would always stand out in a crowd.

There was little if any ceremony about this final stage in a legal process that had begun less than a week earlier. The six condemned men were led to the gallows, assisted up the stairs by their guards, and placed in front of one of the ten nooses attached to a long overhead beam. The carpenters had done a good job; the gallows were actually built in two parts, allowing the six murderers to be hanged in a batch at one end and the four thieves in a batch at the other.

The two priests, Therry and Keane, had accompanied the men but remained at the foot of the gallows which was now also occupied by the condemned men, the hangman — quite probably the flagellator who had kicked the whole thing off almost exactly one year earlier — one or two armed guards, and a court officer who read out the warrant authorising the execution.

As the hangman was beginning to place the nooses over the condemned men's heads, Ralph Entwistle looked down at the crowd gathered below and called to them in a loud voice, that voice betraying no emotion beyond a sense of irony.

"My old mother always said I would die like a brave soldier, with my boots on," he said, *"but I'll make a liar of her yet!"*

And with that he kicked his boots off into the crowd, one after the other.

There was no time for anything else, for by then the hangman had placed and adjusted the nooses around all six necks. He then stepped back and pulled the lever. This removed a large restraining bolt, which caused the trap at the front of the gallows to drop away and brought six men to the end of their earthly journeys.

Fifteen minutes later, a similar procession travelled the short distance from the gaol to the gallows. The process was followed for a second time that morning and a few minutes later, four more bodies joined the six already swaying gently in the breeze. The ten bodies were left hanging there all day, both as a warning to others who might stray and as an example of the terrible majesty of the law. That evening, the ten men were buried in what was to become the first common burial ground in Bathurst, situated on a rise on what was then the western boundary of the settlement. Nine of them were buried in the positions in which their bodies fell when they were lowered to the ground; the tenth was laid carefully on his back, his boots placed carefully on either side of his body.

RIBBON GANG LANE

B athurst changed so much in the decades after the events of 1830 that even someone who returned to the town just 30 years later would have struggled to recognise what they found as being the same place as the settlement they had left. The Bathurst of 1830 was a scattered village comprising both temporary and permanent structures, built of various materials and built for various purposes. There were streets there, but they were routes of convenience rather than planned thoroughfares. The buildings, both permanent and temporary, were located along those streets in a somewhat haphazard manner.

The discovery of gold in many of the region's rivers and creeks had transformed the small settlement into a bustling town 30 years on; one that had doubled, then quadrupled in size and which continued to grow. Another quarter century would see that bustling town become a sedate and comfortable regional centre, with proud buildings of locally-hewn stone and locally-made bricks. The heart of that city would be laid out in a basic grid pattern with the main streets running from the north-east to the south-west, and from the north-west to the south-east. The names of those streets would reflect the history of the city — its pioneers and their patrons, and the officials in Australia and England who had exercised some degree of influence over the town, the region and its inhabitants.

You will find within that grid the names of English kings and Ministers of the Crown, including William and George, and Peel as well. You will also find the names of prominent citizens from the early days of both Sydney and Bathurst: Piper, Keppel and Bentinck. Reflecting their early occupants, there is a Church Street and a Barrack Street and running between Church Street and William Street, is a little curved thoroughfare shaped like an elongated and upside-down letter "L". It is called Ribbon Gang Lane.

*   *   *

Somewhere within the little island of land formed by William and Church Streets and Ribbon Gang Lane is the site of the gallows built to execute Ralph Entwistle and nine of his fellow bushrangers. That site was chosen in part because it was proximate to both the gaol and the courthouse, but the present structures that bear those names are not the originals, nor are they necessarily anywhere near where their 1830 predecessors once stood. The gaol, for instance, was somewhere down William Street from the site of the gallows, but no-one can be certain exactly where it stood. Similarly, the precise location of the original courthouse is unknown, but it must have been somewhere in that general area.

Early records also suggest that the bodies of the bushrangers were buried on the margins of the 1830 settlement, somewhere in the vicinity of what is now the intersection of George and Lambert Streets. The growth of Bathurst made the site too valuable to remain as a cemetery and so the bodies there were disinterred for removal to a new cemetery, believed to have been located at the lower end of Lambert Street. That cemetery, too, would be relocated to a major new cemetery in West Bathurst, one which exists to this day.

The grave digger responsible for the first disinterments later recalled how he had uncovered the bodies of nine men in a row, all still wearing the clothes in which they had been buried. Alongside them was the tenth body, with its boots carefully placed alongside. From that time, around the end of the 1830's, the fate of the remains of the Ribbon Gang is not known. They were presumably removed to the new cemetery at that point, but whether or not they now rest somewhere out at West Bathurst is a mystery, something of which Ralph Entwistle would probably be proud.

*   *   *

A lot more is known about others who were directly involved in the events surrounding Entwistle's little uprising. Thomas Evernden remained as a pastoralist and a magistrate sitting at Bathurst. Such was his savagery in handing down punishments that he became known throughout the district, and the colony, as the flogging magistrate. It was reported that, in one 12-month period, he sentenced 225 men to a total of 12,000 lashes.

Thomas and Mary Jane Evernden's marriage produced four children, three of whom died in infancy. Himself subjected to increasing ill-health, Evernden was forced to resign from both the magistracy and the mounted police. He retired to his farm and its magnificent homestead, Littlebourne, which he had built there, and which today is a popular bed and breakfast resort. Thomas Evernden died at Littlebourne on 15 September 1839 and was buried in the graveyard of the church he had also helped to build, Holy Trinity Church, at Kelso, now part of the greater Bathurst city.

Captain Horatio Walpole continued his service with the 39th Regiment of Foot, in New South Wales, then India and wherever else the regiment served. He later became a major and then a lieutenant colonel, purchasing both commissions when they became available through the retirement of the incumbents. Walpole himself retired as a lieutenant colonel on half pay in 1852.

Lachlan Macalister also continued to serve New South Wales as both a magistrate and as an officer in the New South Wales Mounted Police. In the mid-1830's, he was appointed to the command of the mounted police at Bathurst, replacing Thomas Evernden. Shortly afterwards, Macalister decided it was time to do something for himself. He resigned from his civilian and police positions and in 1837 overlanded to the Port Phillip District, taking up one pastoral run near Geelong and another on the Goulburn River. He also purchased several town lots in Melbourne. It was Macalister who sponsored his clansman, Angus MacMillan, during MacMillan's explorations in Gippsland and in the high country around Omeo. Macalister finally married at Picton in New South Wales in 1851 but died just four years later.

The Suttor family would become increasingly prominent in colonial circles. George Suttor, who would die at Bathurst in 1859, continued his deep interest in both science and farming and the interactions between the two; he had treatises on related subjects published in both Australia and England, where he lived between 1839 and 1845. His son, William, took the potential embarrassment of Grove Creek in his stride, and within 20 years had become one of Australia's largest landholders, owning hundreds of thousands of acres across both New South Wales and Queensland. He also became involved in colonial politics, serving in several ministries in New South Wales' governments, and also becoming quite a local philanthropist in Bathurst. He married in Sydney in 1833, and he and his wife reared ten sons and four daughters, with several of the former also seeking careers in politics. William Suttor died at one of his properties, Captain Piper's old farm, Alloway Bank, near Bathurst in 1877.

George Ranken and his nephew Arthur had the distinction of owning properties which were among the first and last farms ever raided by the Ribbon Gang. Both Rankens also prospered as pastoralists, George primarily in the Bathurst region and Arthur further out on the plains alongside the Lachlan River where the town of Forbes, named after Sir Francis Forbes, now stands. In the late 1830's, George Ranken bought Thomas Icely's property, Saltram, and turned it into one of the show properties in the district. He also returned to Scotland to live. When the Bathurst region was devastated by drought in the early 1840's, Ranken returned to Australia to once again take personal control of his properties. George Ranken died in London in 1860.

It is thought that one of the police troopers, who scoured the Abercrombie Caves complex during the search for the Ribbon Gang in September and October 1830, dropped a set of convict leg irons while doing so. Some 64 years later, the first caretaker of those caves, a man named Sam Grosvenor, discovered those leg irons buried in the mud which formed the floor of one of the caves, which he promptly named Bushrangers' Cave. The leg irons are still on display at the Abercrombie Caves Visitors' Centre.Most of the other features in the bushland that both housed and protected Ralph Entwistle and his gang of bushrangers were either completely obliterated or changed forever 20 years later when thousands of diggers descended on the area following the discovery of gold in its watercourses and in the little hidden valleys where those watercourses arose.

*   *   *

As far as rebellions go, that staged by Entwistle and his Ribbon Gang has been overlooked as being too small, too localised and too unsuccessful, and has therefore been consigned to the margins of history where it is a footnote, if it is noted at all. Despite the brouhaha and hyperbole it generated in some quarters during the three weeks that took it from start to finish, there were no obvious long-term implications to what had taken place out there on the margins of civilization. It caused some minor dislocation in the short term; a number of settlers abandoned their isolated farms while Entwistle and his gang were at large, while supplies of the region's cheese, beef and mutton to Sydney were temporarily disrupted.

There were, however, some lessons to be learned from the affair, but only by those who could view the colonial society in which it occurred with a degree of objectivity, something which is not always evident in contemporary reporting of Ralph Entwistle and his exploits. As a transported convict, Entwistle was probably little different from thousands of other convicts until that hot November day beside the river near Bathurst. For him and for those who joined him, Entwistle's rebellion or uprising — call it what you will — was a crude response to arbitrary punishment being bestowed on personal whims. It was about power and the application of power by those who wield it. But most of all it was about fairness and proportionality, and fourteen people would die in Ralph Entwistle's attempt to very publicly make those points. His was an enterprise doomed to failure from the time the scheme was first hatched, but for Entwistle and the Ribbon Gang of Bathurst, they were points and principles worth dying for.

THE
GREAT
BEYOND

The Horrocks of
Penworthham Hall

I f the aim of the founders and promoters of the new colony of South
Australia was to attract English "gentlemen" to their little settlement at the other end of the world, the Horrocks of Penwortham
Hall, Lancashire, would have been high on their list. The Horrocks did
not (yet) represent either a long-established landed gentry or wealth and
influence linked to royal connections, but they had both money and
drive, qualities that were more valuable in South Australia than a substantial entry in Debrett's Peerage or an ability to trace a lineage directly
back to some minor Norman knight.

Instead, the Horrocks represented new money, and new money in
Lancashire in the opening decades of the 19th Century was inevitably
linked to the Industrial Revolution and specifically to the textiles trade.
For the Horrocks, that textile was cotton and Horrocks' Cotton Mill
had become one of the country's leading mills by 1820. Success brought
John Horrocks, the youngest son of 18 children born to a Quaker family
and the driving force behind the family's rise, real wealth and, with that
wealth, political connections. Those connections saw John Horrocks
returned as the Member of Parliament for Preston at several elections,
whilst his wealth enabled him to build Penwortham Hall.

Penwortham Hall's main house, outbuildings, paddocks and fields were certainly something to behold. Penwortham Hall itself was a large, solid stone house set on a hill which commanded sweeping views of the surrounding countryside. One vista looked across to the venerable Penwortham Abbey Church; a neighbouring hill was crowned by Houghton Tower, a fortified manor house and grounds dating back to the 12th Century. Another hill had been taken over by the bustling town of Preston while below all this the Ribble River bounced and bubbled westward to the Irish Sea.

Penwortham Hall was a substantial edifice by any reckoning. It possessed a large entry hall, an even larger dining room, a library containing 30,000 books and a long hallway which ended in enormous sliding mahogany doors which opened onto a well-furnished drawing room. There were bedrooms and bathrooms and dressing rooms, all beautifully furnished, and there were also underground kitchens, lobbies, storerooms, cellars, a scullery, a pantry and even a gun room.

Clustered around the main building were a number of smaller buildings, all providing the services necessary to support and maintain a small village, which is what Penwortham Hall really was. The stables were almost as large as the main building. Built of brick as well, they contained individual stalls for 12 horses, loose boxes for extra stock, a harness room, a hayloft and a coach house. There was also a brewery, a laundry, a washhouse and a cowhouse with stalls for six cows. The training and exercise yard attached to the stables was almost 100 metres in length, half as wide again, and was surrounded by a high brick wall which contained double folding entry gates. The entire complex was screened from view by a plantation of oak and elm trees.

The entire property covered around 18 hectares (40 acres), and aside from the main and subsidiary buildings also contained shrubberies, ornamental works, flower gardens and tree plantations. All the fields were surrounded by hedgerows while, near the main residence, there was a walled-in orchard. Finally, there were cottages for the butler and the gardener, each of which had its own attached garden.

A large staff was required to keep the whole Penwortham Hall enterprise going. That staff comprised a butler, two footmen, a "boots", a cook, a nursery governess, a needlewoman, a scullery maid, a coach man, three stable boys, a groom, a head gardener and six labourers.

*   *   *

When John Horrocks died in 1804 (some thought from overwork), he left Penwortham Hall and an estate valued at 60,000 pounds to his son, Peter. Control of the Horrocks' cotton milling operations remained with Samuel Horrocks, John's younger brother whom he had brought into the business. Peter Horrocks was only 13 years old when his father died, and he continued down the educational path that his father had planned for him. He studied at both Rugby School and Oxford University, where he made something of a name for himself as a good Latin, Greek and German scholar, while he had also spoken French fluently from an early age. Six feet tall, and a keen sportsman, Peter Horrocks could have almost been the archetype of the English country gentleman.

In 1811, the then 20-year-old Peter Horrocks married Clara Jerr It seems to have been a love match, although Clara's family was another which had won eminence and wealth during the Industrial Revolution. Children soon blessed the union. Four daughters named Clara, Celia, Augusta and Alicia arrived before a son and heir was born on 22 March 1818. They named the boy John Ainsworth Horrocks; John for his paternal grandfather and Ainsworth for his mother's family home. John's birth was followed by the arrival of three more boys, Arthur, Eustace and William, all born at Penwortham Hall. There would be other children, another boy and another girl, but they would be born elsewhere because, when they were delivered, Penwortham Hall was no longer the family home.

In July 1829, Peter Horrocks sold Penwortham Hall for a large sum of money — 150,000 pounds was mentioned — and moved his young and growing family to London. The ostensible reason for the move was to be closer to the Horrocks' family counting house, the financial centre of the family's various textile-based enterprises. They moved into a substantial townhouse adjacent to Regent's Park, and it was there that the family narrowly avoided a tragedy.

Regent's Park was a magnet to the Horrocks' children, summer and winter. One winter's day, just as John and Arthur were entering their teens (there was only a year between them), the boys went ice-skating on one of the frozen ponds in the park. As they and their friends skated across the ice, it gave way and John crashed through into the chilly water below. He was immediately in trouble, and it looked like other parts of the ice were also too thin to support any real weight.

Quick thinking by Arthur fashioned a rescue. Lying on the ice, he slid over to where John was struggling and, when he was as near as he dared go, stretched out his hand to his brother, helping John to keep his head above water. Other, stronger boys and young men then also stretched out across the ice, forming a human chain between solid ground and the boy struggling in the water. Eventually, both Horrocks' boys were dragged to safety, but the rescue came at a price. As the human chain was pulling Arthur and John to safety, the force needed was such that one of Arthur's legs was badly dislocated in the process. Despite what must have been unbelievable pain for a boy, Arthur's hold on his brother never loosened.

John Horrocks quickly recovered from the shock he had suffered. Arthur Horrocks was not so lucky. He was confined to bed for 13 months and walked with crutches for a further three years. He would be lame in that leg for the rest of his life.

*   *   *

Peter Horrocks' own health began to decline after the family moved to London and, perhaps on medical advice, he moved the family again, this time to continental Europe. After living in several chateaux in France, the family finally settled in one near Boulogne, where Clara gave birth to another daughter. Peter had earlier befriended Prince Paul Esterhazy in London when the Hungarian had been the Habsburg Empire's ambassador to Great Britain. From Boulogne, he accepted Esterhazy's invitation to relocate once again, this time to a villa outside Vienna, where the family would remain for three years and where Clara would give birth to another son, who they christened Crawford.

John Horrocks was not part of that move to Vienna. The senior Horrocks decided that when they moved to Vienna in 1834, John would attend school in Paris. He would board at the school they selected and family friends, Sir Charles and Lady Rich who resided in Paris, would be able to keep an eye on him while he studied. Like the rest of the children, John had been home tutored since the family left England, and he struggled to settle into the strict routine the French school imposed on him. It all came to a head when a schoolmaster slapped him for some real or imagined infraction of the rules. John struck back and knocked the schoolmaster to the ground.

His punishment was immediate. John was taken to a small garret set aside for transgressors. He would stay there, locked in and subsisting on a diet of bread and water, until the headmaster believed that he had learned his lesson. John had already learned the lesson, though, and as soon as he was left alone, he began to prepare an escape, which he carried out with a real sense of urgency. Almost as soon as the key had turned in the lock, John was figuring out a way to break out of the room, which he soon did. Within hours, he had also run away from the school and was hitching his way across France. In his pocket he carried all the money he possessed, a five-franc piece.

John travelled first to Geneva, where he visited a family friend from the Horrocks' stay at Boulogne, a Captain Tweeddale, who welcomed him into his home, fussed over him for a few days, then loaned him 50 pounds so he could continue his journey in more comfort than had so far been the case. Several weeks after he left Paris, John arrived at the Horrocks' villa in Vienna. Had he taken a direct route, he would have travelled just on 1200 kilometres, but his detour to Geneva probably doubled the distance. A seasoned traveller would have struggled to do better, and John was not yet the voyager he would become; he was just 16 years old.

*   *   *

The Horrocks do not seem to have done anything in Vienna beyond enjoying everything that the great city offered. They were all well-received at the Austrian Court and when Esterhazy was made Lord Lieutenant of Hungary, Peter, John and his four older sisters holidayed at the Royal Palace in Budapest for two weeks. Their lives followed the seasonal rhythms of the Imperial Court; high and low social seasons, and regular holidays in such places as Trieste and Gorizia. John became acquainted with all the young nobility in Vienna, which was a particular paradise for the older Horrocks girls.

Crawford Horrocks was born in Vienna, limiting the opportunities for Peter and Clara to pursue some of the opportunities that were placed in front of their older children. John had already demonstrated his self-reliance, and so he was called upon to act as chaperone to the older Horrocks girls as they made several excursions into the countryside. On one occasion, an excursion became an expedition, and John escorted his sisters to, from and around Venice. As he approached his 18th birthday, John was asked to join Prince Paul Esterhazy's personal bodyguard or to accept a post in the Austrian Army but, in truth, neither offer appealed to him. Fortunately, he did not have to make a decision as Peter Horrocks had decided to relocate his family; again.

*   *   *

In 1836, Peter announced that the family would return to England, and would again live in London. Furthermore, he and his daughter Alicia would go first while 18-year-old John would finalise their affairs in Vienna and then escort his mother and siblings to London. The first part of those instructions was completed without much ado, but the return to London turned into something of a grand tour. In an assortment of carriages and charabancs, the Horrocks' travelled slowly, but in style, via the Italian Alps and the Tyrol, via Innsbruck, Bavaria — including a short stay in Munich — to Prussia, and then back to Frankfurt before travelling via Amsterdam to Rotterdam where they caught the steamship *Batavia* to London.

In London, Peter and Alicia Horrocks had taken possession of a large house in Berkeley Square, and it was there that the family resided for the next two and a half years. Peter then moved his family once again, this time a much shorter journey to the town of Chertsey in Surrey on London's fringe. There he purchased a property known as Richmond House. Almost as large as Penwortham Hall, it would remain the family home until Peter's death. That was some time into the future, though, and their return to London had brought into stark relief an issue of more immediacy; just what would the older Horrocks boys do with their lives?

*   *   *

It was almost immediately evident that John's great uncle Samuel, head of the Horrocks' milling operations, would not welcome him into the family firm. There seem to have been unstated assumptions that John was, perhaps, a bit too modern, too bohemian and worldly after his adventures in Europe. The London Horrocks do not seem to have been too perturbed by this snub from their Lancashire relatives, probably because their energies were now being focussed on a new venture on the other side of the world.

South Australia had officially proclaimed itself a colony on 28 December 1836, and its 636 British colonists and their financial supporters back home hoped that it would soon become another jewel in the British Crown. South Australia would be different to the other settlements the British had established on Australia's eastern seaboard at Hobart and Launceston, Sydney and Brisbane. To begin with, there would be no convicts sent to the colony, meaning it would never be tainted by the convict stain which attached to those other settlements.

South Australia would also be a colony established on the then rather modern concept of tolerance. Its tolerance would extend to religious, social, economic and political beliefs, and foreigners seeking that tolerance would also be encouraged to move to South Australia. It would also be a self-funding colony based on the ideas of Edward Wakefield, a former diplomat and convicted child abductor. The London-based promoter believed land sales in his proposed colony of South Australia could finance its development, as those who bought the land at a fair price would have to improve that land to turn a profit, and the process of improvement would inevitably attract both artisans and labourers to the colony. The Wakefield scheme was elegant in its simplicity.

It was also attractive to Peter Horrocks, a man of considerable means who also had a number of sons approaching their majority but with no real prospects in sight. Peter seems to have become aware of South Australia and the scheme underpinning its development almost as soon as he returned to London and found it a most attractive proposition. His older daughter, Clara, had also learned of, and been impressed by the project; family lore has it that she learned of South Australia when visiting relatives of the Rothschild's.

After some discussions within the family, in which John seemed particularly enthusiastic, Peter Horrocks determined to invest in the fledgling colony. He put up 10,000 pounds to be used to purchase land in South Australia and to outfit and transport a small group of pioneer settlers. That group would sail to South Australia, take up the land he had bought there, and establish an enterprise much like the one he had inherited at Penwortham Hall, but on a larger scale. One of his sons, the 16-year-old Eustace, would be one of the party, which would be led by his eldest son, John Ainsworth Horrocks.

*   *   *

John worked hard to put together an emigrant party, plus all the supplies and equipment they would need to establish a working property in South Australia. That party would comprise 20 or more people, and among the first of them were two brothers he had known in his youth: John and Edwin Green, both of Penwortham Hall. John Green had been, and remained, Peter Horrocks' butler, while Edwin had been the head gardener at Penwortham Hall. Both agreed to join the Horrocks' emigrant party. A number of shepherds and labourers who had been at Penwortham Hall were also approached and most signed up for the enterprise immediately. A stricture on single male shepherds saw one young shepherd marry before offering his own, and his wife's services.

Tools and all the equipment needed to build a small estate were purchased and warehoused until they were ready to depart. Similarly, seeds of a wide variety of trees, grasses, fruit and vegetables were bought and stored, as were sundry items like clocks, cutlery and crockery, napery and even a large church bell. The party would also take its own livestock, although this would be limited to prime breeding stock as they believed they could purchase further stock and supplies when they arrived in South Australia. Rounding out their cargo, this livestock comprised four prime Merino rams, several sheepdogs and a couple of greyhounds.

On the eve of his departure for South Australia, John's sister and closest confidante, Celia, described her brother as, "a remarkably brave, strong, active, affectionate and upright-minded boy". Shortly afterwards, John, his brother Eustace, their emigrant party and all their equipment and supplies were loaded aboard the *Catherine Stuart Forbes* at St. Katharine Dock in London. The 457-ton ship, which had been used to carry convicts to Australia in 1830 and 1832, was under the command of Captain Alfred Fell. On the outgoing tide on 20 October 1838, Fell ordered the lines to be cast and the voyage to the other side of the world began.

It was a voyage all would remember. Shortly after sailing, the ship was caught in a number of storms in the English Channel and out in the Atlantic. It took six weeks to cover a distance it would normally have covered in one. This led to a shortage of fresh water aboard when they were well out into the Atlantic. Fortunately, when they were approaching the coast of America, they fell in with another ship which was able to supply them with both lemons and water.

John Horrocks proved to be a popular shipboard companion, and this, too, led to some problems at sea. Eustace Horrocks was not in good health. He was variously described as "prissy" and weak in both body and mind; John himself once called Eustace a "fop". During the voyage, John became firm friends with the ship's surgeon and his wife and, perhaps through jealousy or perhaps through spite, Eustace accused John of having a liaison with the doctor's wife. John was outraged by the allegation, seizing Eustace by the throat and shaking him vigorously.

Eustace survived both the punishment and the journey and was standing alongside his brother when the *Catherine Stuart Forbes* dropped anchor in Holdfast Bay, just off the coast of South Australia and a little below Adelaide. It was five months and two days since they departed England, and the date was 22 March 1839. That was John Horrocks' 21st birthday; he was legally a man, and he was ready to start a new life in a new land.

NORTH

A number of the residents of the bustling little town of Adelaide, now growing quite rapidly along the banks of the Torrens River, were immediately impressed when they met John Horrocks. Contemporary reports described the young man as being 6 feet 3 inches (190 cm) in height, handsome and with an oval face enclosed by a mass of dark brown curls. Some went even further, noting that he was, "*a handsome young fellow, with fine large eyes and a mouth which speaks both of gentleness and determination*".

These qualities of gentleness and determination were to be sorely tested from the time John Horrocks first came ashore in South Australia.

In England, Peter Horrocks had purchased and paid for 1000 acres of land in South Australia and had also appointed John Morphett, one of the promoters of the colonisation scheme, as his agent in Adelaide. Morphett met John Horrocks and his party soon after they had disembarked, and gave the young man the news that, while the land purchase was all fair and above board, the land itself was not yet available to be taken up. The reason for this, Morphett explained, was that it had not yet been surveyed. With so many settlers arriving to take up the land they had purchased, the system had broken down. No-one was certain when the backlog would be cleared, but until then, John and his party should take up temporary quarters and familiarise themselves with Adelaide and its environs.

That was only ever going to be a short-term fix for the restless John Horrocks, and as the weeks became months, he grew increasingly frustrated. He knew that the best land around Adelaide, including the hills and valleys which hemmed the settlement in to the east had already been claimed, which meant that his land was going to be either beyond the Adelaide Hills/Mount Lofty Ranges barrier, or in a place some distance to the north of Adelaide. With this in mind, John sought out anyone who could tell him just what was out there. One of those he spoke to was another young man just three years older than himself, Edward John Eyre.

Eyre had already made a name for himself in Adelaide. In early 1838, he had arrived at the South Australian capital after overlanding several hundred sheep and cattle from his property, Woodlands, on the Molonglo Plains in southern New South Wales. With the proceeds from the sale of the livestock, he returned to Woodlands, restocked and repeated the exercise, bringing 1000 sheep and 600 cattle overland to Adelaide in early 1839. Funds from the sale of those livestock allowed Eyre to indulge in his passion for exploration. In May 1839, Eyre and a small party travelled north from Adelaide, hoping to open up the interior of the colony. Well beyond the limits of settlement, their way was blocked by a huge body of water which Eyre named Lake Torrens. From his base on a small watercourse he called Depot Creek, Eyre pushed out in several directions, finding little, before returning to Adelaide. Shortly afterwards, he was introduced to John Horrocks.

Eyre told the young Englishman that he had been particularly impressed by the country he had found some two days' riding, or over 100 miles, to the north of Adelaide. John Hill, Eyre's friend and a fellow explorer, had first passed through the area in April 1839 and thought it offered excellent potential for pastoral activities. Hill had called the general area Wakefield, after the architect of the colonisation scheme, and the main river which flowed through the area the Hutt River after one of the scheme's principal English backers. Eyre had passed through that same area just a month after Hill, and had found grassy valleys and timbered hills, well-watered by a chain of large ponds which would coalesce into streams after good rains. That country continued some distance to the north, where it included the Broughton River, which Eyre had discovered and named after the Anglican Bishop of Australia. Eyre had gone as far north as he dared, beyond the head of Spencer's Gulf, to a point where his way was blocked by the saltwaters of Lake Torrens. He had made a base camp, he told Horrocks, on a small creek containing permanent springs which he had used as a depot and called Depot Creek. At a future date, he hoped to continue exploring beyond that point.

John Horrocks was intrigued by everything he heard. His own future lay in the north, he was certain, and he couldn't wait to get started.

*   *   *

Within days, Horrocks had organised a trip to the area which had so impressed both Hill and Eyre. Taking just John Green and enough supplies to keep the men and their horses going for several days, he headed north, using a compass for direction by day and the stars at night. Horrocks and Green travelled for two and a half days before finding a spot that Horrocks judged as being exceedingly suitable. Situated in the upper reaches of the Hutt River valley, it offered both grasslands and timbered slopes plus a permanent water supply. Not wanting to risk losing such pastures, Horrocks sent John Green back to Adelaide to start the others on the trip and to guide them to the place they had found. He would stay in the valley until the others arrived; he had found an enormous gum tree with part of its trunk hollowed out by Aboriginals using fire. The space within was large enough to store supplies, and he could even sleep inside, if necessary.

John told Green to urge the others to hurry, as such rich country would not remain unoccupied for long. He also said to tell Eustace and the others that he had chosen a name for their settlement; it would be called Penwortham.

*   *   *

The hollow tree was to serve as a home for John Horrocks for the two weeks it took Eustace, John Green and the others to make their way north to the new Penwortham. He cooked and laundered in it during the day and slept inside it at night. The baggage that arrived with the settlers' party included several tents, and those became the accommodation for the settlers until something more permanent could be built. Back in Adelaide the formal process of acquiring title to the land that Horrocks had occupied began, and on 2 December 1839, Peter Horrocks — as the principal financier — paid an additional 2000 pounds and deeded 25 land orders of 80 acres each, taking possession of 15,000 acres in total. This vast property included Hope Farm, the name John had given to his pastoral run; Penwortham Farm and village; the Hutt River station; and Eyre Creek, a watercourse which flowed through the area to the Hutt River.

At Penwortham, work proceeded on several fronts. Their first task was to cut timber for the corrals and paddocks they would need for the livestock they already had and for the livestock that John was planning to purchase to stock the entire run. There were store sheds and stables to be built, and timbered areas to be cleared and then prepared for crops and orchards. John Horrocks worked tirelessly alongside his English labourers, as well as the occasional Aboriginal who could be enticed to work with the promise of a few plugs of tobacco. The only one who took no part was Eustace Horrocks, who had grown increasingly frail.

John had an awning built for Eustace, and the fragile young man sat there day after day, uncomplaining, as a large farm and a small village were built right before his eyes. As day followed day, a pattern of sorts was established. The one large tent they had became the focus of the settlement, serving as both a dining room and a recreation area. Every evening, dinner would be served there, commencing when John sat down behind his solid silver cutlery at the head of the main table. Every Sunday morning, all would gather in the tent to hear John read them the morning church service. Sunday afternoon was given over to riding, shooting and whatever other forms of recreation or sport appealed to the men.

John also had his men start to build permanent housing, including a small stone cottage at Hope Farm, which he would move into before the winter of 1840. By then, the farms around it and the village of Penwortham itself were assuming an air of permanence, and John himself was able to look a bit further into the future. Eustace's health was such that John doubted whether he would live much longer. The brothers agreed that Eustace should return to England, where at least the care he would receive would be immeasurably better than anything he could expect to find on the Australian frontier. He returned to England during 1840, and he would die there in 1844.

One of the tasks John had set himself was to build up the stock carrying capacity of the various properties he had an interest in, and he was almost immediately successful in this. As soon as the basic infrastructure was complete, John began purchasing stock that had been overlanded from New South Wales by entrepreneurs like Edward Eyre. To improve the quality of that livestock, he imported stud bulls and rams, like the four Windsor Park Merino rams he bought in 1840.

The success of his approach was soon apparent. To try to keep the South Australian sheep flocks free from disease, a "Scab in Sheep" Act had been passed early in the colony's development and this act required pastoralists to complete an annual return of sheep numbers. John Horrocks' return for August 1841 showed that, halfway through its second full year of operation, Hope Farm was carrying 500 male and 3000 female sheep. By then, he was employing more than 20 people on his farm and had just added a stockyard capable of holding more than 1500 cattle; John would always think large.

John's success had also come about through a combination of hard work and fortuitous circumstances. The colonisation of South Australia did not proceed as quickly or as well as Wakefield and his backers had hoped, and in its first few years, the colony's fortunes swung between boom and bust. John Horrocks returned to Adelaide regularly during his first two years in the north, gaining firsthand knowledge of this pendulum. He would travel to the town to purchase supplies, arrange for the importation of some things and the export of others. If he was alone with just his horse and his dog, he would make the journey in two days each way; if he took a dray, it would double or treble the travelling time, depending on the season, the state of the track and the weight of the load his dray was carrying.

Every time he went to Adelaide, John found prices higher than they had been on the previous visit; it was not unusual to pay sixpence or more for a single egg, a price unheard of anywhere else, where sixpence would buy a dozen. He also found on several trips that there were numbers of settlers waiting, just as he had, for the land they had purchased from the colony's agents in London to be surveyed and released to them. He was able to coax some of them to join him at Penwortham, to work on the various properties there while they waited for their own to be made available. Those who agreed to join him would have their debts paid by John, who would also finance their journey to the north.

Collecting and reading the mail awaiting him, and despatching his own, served as a reminder that he was part of a much larger family, and part of a much larger world.

*   *   *

The departure of John and Eustace Horrocks to South Australia in October 1838 was not the only change in the Horrocks family. Around the same time, 18-year-old Arthur Horrocks was also sent from the family home in Chertsey to find his way in the world. He first went north, to a textile spinning mill in Lancashire, where he spent six months learning the intricacies of the textiles trade and the yarn spinning industry. From Lancashire, Arthur moved across the Channel to Antwerp, where he worked at a trading house studying and learning the way of international trade.

Like his older brother, Arthur was apparently not satisfied with a sedentary life, and after almost two years in Antwerp he, too, decided to try his luck on the other side of the world. Arthur, though, chose Mauritius. It was while living there that Arthur learned that Eustace had returned to England in poor health. Such a possibility must have been foreseen as, in line with a promise Arthur had made to his mother, he left Mauritius to join John in South Australia. His rambling journey included lengthy stopovers in Sydney, Melbourne and Hobart, before Arthur finally landed at Port Adelaide in February 1841.

Arthur spent a few days in Adelaide where he contacted a merchant named Abraham Davis, who was then acting as John's agent in the town, as well as several more of John's acquaintances and business associates. He then set off in a small carriage for Penwortham, accompanied by an Aboriginal who had overlanded from New South Wales. Their buggy broke down just 30 kilometres short of Penwortham, but they were able to get a message through to Hope Farm. John Green came to their rescue and they eventually reached the farm and the village at 3am to find John Horrocks waiting up for them.

*   *   *

The success of Hope Farm and the arrival of his brother allowed John time to pursue other interests. The first of these was ensuring that all the land he had acquired in the Hutt Valley was given legal recognition; he had seen and heard of too many cases where landholders like himself had lost everything when latecomers challenged their legal right to the land they occupied and the courts found in favour of the latecomers. John had the opportunity to push his own and his neighbours' cases later in 1841 when South Australia's second governor, George Gawler, made a tour of the northern limits of settlement in the colony, and stayed for a couple of days with the Horrocks brothers at Penwortham.

John took the opportunity the visit provided to escort Governor Gawler to the top of Mount Horrocks, the tallest hill in that part of the Hutt Valley. The Governor was on horseback, John on foot, and as they ascended, John pointed out the notable features of the surrounding countryside. He also took the opportunity to discuss such issues as land laws, squatters' rights, and the slow process of acquiring legal title with the Governor. The two men debated a number of contentious points but at the summit of the hill, John Horrocks stopped talking. He had not run out of argument, he told the Governor; he had simply run out of breath.

Those arguments may or may not have worked, or perhaps the system finally caught up with itself. Either way, by 1842, the Horrocks' had legal title to all the land that John had taken up in 1839 and 1840.

*   *   *

John Horrocks' other interest was in what lay around and ahead of him. He may have been inspired by Edward Eyre's descriptions of pushing ever further into the unknown or he may have simply had a curious cast of mind; either way, he always wanted to know what was on the other side of the mountain. His early explorations were small scale and local. Soon after the rest of his party had arrived from Adelaide, John took to riding off, alone except for his dogs, exploring up and down the Hutt River valley. He scaled and named the nearest tall hills to his embryonic settlement, thereby giving Mount Horrocks and Mount Oakden the names they carry to this day.

He thoroughly explored the region around the present-day town of Clare, but his vision was increasingly drawn to the north. He and two others, possibly John Green and John Oakden, pushed up to Eyre's Broughton River and across it to the beautiful rolling country beyond. He named that country the Gulnare Plains, that being the name of his favourite dog, a greyhound. While they were crossing the region, Gulnare had brought down several emus, keeping Horrocks and his companions in fresh meat. He indulged this growing passion even when he travelled to Adelaide. If Eyre was in town, he would seek him out; otherwise he would speak to anyone else he thought could advance his knowledge of the north of the colony. At one time, he even sailed across to Port Lincoln to find out what the locals knew of their hinterland.

John Horrocks may have been hatching plans to either join or try to match his friend Edward Eyre's expeditions as 1841 wound down. If so, those plans were put on hold. Peter Horrocks' health finally gave out and he died at home on 7 June 1841 at just 50 years of age. The news took several months to reach John at Penwortham and when it did, it was accompanied by a message from John's mother. John was needed at home, and could he please come quickly.

*   *   *

John Horrocks' return to England, to his grieving family there, could hardly be described as quick. He spent the first six months of 1842 putting the affairs of Hope Farm and Penwortham village into some kind of order, perhaps conscious of the fact that he might not return. He bought another flock of sheep that had been overlanded from New South Wales, paying the premium price of 30 shillings a head. That purchase took his flock numbers to 9000, and he also left behind a substantial number of both cattle and horses. He left, as well, a vineyard, an orchard, a substantial stone cottage and detailed instructions for three people. One was his brother, Arthur, who he left in charge of Hope Farm; the second was John Oakden, who he named as his land agent; and the third was a Mr. Campbell, who John nominated as his city agent.

Horrocks eventually departed Adelaide on 31 January 1842 aboard the brig *Dorset*. It seems to have been a leisurely return trip. The *Dorset* stopped in Sydney before continuing via Van Diemen's Land and New Zealand to Valparaiso in Chile. There, Horrocks switched ships, continuing to London via Cape Horn aboard a Dutch ship. It was almost the middle of the year before he arrived "home".

When he was back with his family at Richmond House, and after the usual period of catching up with each other's news, Clara Horrocks told her son that she had concerns about her late husband's estate. After the family had moved to Chertsey, Peter Horrocks had met a man named Harry Baldwin, and the two had soon become firm friends. So much so, in fact, that Peter Horrocks had made Baldwin the executor of his will. Now, Clara told her son, Harry Baldwin had gone missing and she had no real idea about the shape of the family's finances. John's investigations soon revealed that Harry Baldwin had indeed helped himself to 10,000 pounds from the Horrocks' estate before fleeing to Paris, where the trail went cold. There was enough left for the family to live comfortably, if not extravagantly.

Apart from looking to his family's future, John had two further tasks he wanted to complete before he departed England. The first was to raise enough money to build a church at Penwortham. He engaged his sister Celia as an assistant and set to with a passion. He sometimes opened his appeal to potential donors by telling the story of how they had constructed a small building in Penwortham with the intention that it would one day become a mill. Until they had the machinery they needed for that purpose, they used the building as a community facility, including holding Sunday church services there. One Saturday night, an unfriendly squatter stabled his horses in the building because of inclement weather. The smell forced the Sunday morning congregation to worship outside in the open. During the following week, the Horrocks and John Jacobs, one of their neighbours and friends, had built a wattle and daub hut for church services, but it was never intended to be anything other than a stop-gap measure.

John and Celia had a mixed response to their fund-raising efforts. The family agreed to provide a residence and financial support to a minister and would also donate six and a half acres of land next to the block in the village which had been set aside for a church; the land they donated was to be used as a cemetery. The northern branch of the Horrocks was less generous, and do not appear to have made any kind of financial donation at all. A cousin on their mother's side listened to John's story and gave him the machinery necessary to build and operate a flour mill. Unfortunately, when they tried to put it together in South Australia, they found that some of the wheels and parts did not fit, so it was never used.

The Society for the propagation of the Gospel and the Society for the Propagation of Christian Knowledge each contributed 100 pounds, and Baroness Burdett-Coutts, an heiress and reputedly England's richest woman, gave 25 pounds. However, she had previously given a lot more than that to establish the Anglican See of Adelaide. All up, around 1400 pounds was collected to build and staff an Anglican church at Penwortham. The money was forwarded to the Anglican Bishop of Sydney, who would hold onto it for as long as he could.

John's second objective in England was to try to raise funds for an expedition to explore deep into the interior of South Australia, something which was becoming increasingly important to him. He made an official approach to the Royal Geographic Society seeking funds to underwrite the expedition in the same way as they had supported several others. The Society did not even respond to his request. Undeterred by the setback, he turned his attention now to his family. It seems his sisters, principally Celia, contributed to his fundraising, and he had 300 pounds to work with almost immediately. Before he could collect more, he received several messages from South Australia, all of them saying the same thing; the bottom had fallen out of the local economy and he was needed back at Penwortham as soon as possible. John tied up as many loose ends as he could before taking passage on the next ship going directly to South Australia. He arrived back in Adelaide on 30 March 1844.

*   *   *

After John had left Penwortham, Arthur Horrocks and John Oakden continued with the broad work plan that he had outlined for them. Part of that plan involved the construction of a more substantial farmhouse at Hope Farm. To assist them in this, they drafted in another of those characters who often emerged in the various outposts of Empire. His name was John Henry Theakston, and he came from one of England's most talented artistic families. John was a sculptor and a sculptor of note. Born in 1809, by 1832 his works were being exhibited at the Royal Academy. Yet by 1838 he was in Adelaide looking around for something to do. He seems to have worked as a mason, and it was in this capacity that he was employed at Penwortham.

Starting late in 1842, Arthur, Oakden, Theakston and several labourers worked on the farmhouse Arthur would name "Wambunga" at Hope Farm. The men quarried the stones needed to build the house, burned the limestone to provide the lime they would need to help cement those stones together, laid the foundations and built the house from the ground up. The walls were raised, a roof put on and the window frames filled with glass brought up from Adelaide. It took them eight months to complete the building, with its four main rooms and associated outbuildings, but they built it to last. John Theakston carved the Horrocks' family crest and motto, "By Hope", in the lintel above the main door, and the building was complete.

Theakston returned to Adelaide, where he took over the Beulah Hotel in Walkerville, while Arthur and Oakden continued their work at Hope Farm. They fenced one of their 50-acre allotments, and there planted a wheat crop that would produce top quality wheat for years to come. As they continued to work through John Horrocks' plan for the farm and village, that plan had its base undercut. South Australia had entered one of its bust cycles and the local economy there crashed. Credit was the first casualty, with everyone from retailers to farm workers demanding that they now be paid with cash.

Hope Farm and Penwortham were not immune from the cash crisis, and the only way that Arthur and Oakden could see their way to continue was to sell off their prime asset, their livestock. The flock of 9000 sheep was reduced to just a couple of hundred of their best breeding stock. Sheep that John had paid 30 shillings for after they had been brought from New South Wales were now off-loaded for three shillings each.

It was root and branch surgery, but it was necessary, and it did mean that when John returned to Penwortham in April 1844, he had something to return to. John and Arthur would have to rebuild the Horrocks' dream, but this time they would not be building from scratch.

A Camel Named Harry

Somewhere, and at some time between leaving England and the end of the year it took him to sort out the mess he found when he returned to Penwortham, John Horrocks decided to give up his plan of becoming some kind of antipodean Lord of the Manor in the valley of the Hutt River. It had all been part of a wider dream, and probably not even his dream at that, this plan to recreate Penwortham Hall at the limits of settlement in South Australia. For one, the endless landscapes of the interior of Australia simply did not lend themselves to the English manorial system of which Penwortham Hall was just, for the Horrocks, another, more recent example of something that had lasted for centuries. For another, John Horrocks was never going to be "M'Lord", the gentleman in the big house on the hill, keeping a benign eye on the peasants toiling in the fields below. That was not him, and that was not his style. John was a doer, not a watcher, and what he increasingly wanted to do was push ever further into that endless landscape.

When he returned to Hope Farm and Penwortham, he realised that blame for what had happened could be not apportioned to anyone in the Hutt Valley. The disaster that struck there was simply the local iteration of the disaster that had struck the colony as a whole. To John, it was just another example of how precarious farming could be where the climate — both literal and financial — was subject to the vagaries of both human and Mother Nature. It was an activity, a lifestyle and life choice he could admire in others but was not one that he would choose for himself. John was ever the realist, so he knew that running an enormous pastoral operation while overseeing the development of a small village was not something the Australian Horrocks would ever be suited to. John's temperament was too mercurial; the challenges a pastoralist faced too mundane for his liking. Arthur's lameness made him unsuited physically to the outdoor life of a grazier; intellectually, and by inclination, Arthur was a businessman whose natural habitat was the city and the hubble and bubble of counting houses and banks.

Once those simple truths were recognised, the rest was easy. While the Horrocks would remain the owners of all they had worked so hard to build, they would no longer be owner occupiers. Their various properties were leased out when suitable tenants were found. John Green took over one of the Hutt Valley runs, Hope Farm itself was let and an agent, Mr. E. C. Gwynne — a lawyer specialising in property law — was appointed to make sure that all the payments and financial obligations were met. John and Arthur would stay in the Hope Farm homestead until other accommodation was arranged. The new arrangements promised to return to John at least 300 pounds a year in rental income and freed him up to focus on other projects.

He had not forgotten one of the tasks he had promised to undertake when he had been in England, that of establishing an Anglican church in Penwortham, and he moved to bring that to fruition as soon as he could. John Jacobs remained his partner in this, and the two men worked to have the funds John had collected released by the authorities in Sydney, while also arranging for the minister's position to be advertised in both England and Australia.

Sites were surveyed, church designs commissioned, and the long, slow process begun.

John now turned his attention to what he really wanted to do, and that was to explore the interior of South Australia and, in particular, the country to the north-west of the top of Spencer Gulf. The main and stated aim of these explorations was to see whether there was land suitable for sheep and/ or cattle runs in that direction, but Horrocks had other objectives as well. In 1840/41, his friend Edward Eyre had made one of his great treks into the unknown when he crossed from South Australia to Albany in Western Australia, skirting the Great Australian Bight and coming close to death several times as he did so. If a more suitable, inland route could be found, both Western and South Australia would benefit. Finally, there was the challenge of pushing on, going to places where no other European had been.

The area he chose to explore certainly fitted the latter category. When Eyre had pushed directly north from Adelaide in 1839, he had found his way completely blocked by the enormous body of saltwater that he had named Lake Torrens. More recently, in the latter half of 1844, Charles Sturt and a well-equipped party of 15 men and supplies — which included 200 sheep and a boat — had attempted to explore what lay beyond Lake Torrens by pushing past it on the east before driving back to the north-west and onwards, towards the centre of the continent. Sturt and his party travelled via the Murray and Darling Rivers to the point where Sturt decided to go inland. It was no good; the party encountered a stony desert and unbelievable heat, so were forced back.

John Horrocks' plans were on a lesser scale, in that he would make a modest attempt to skirt Lake Torrens to the west, only going as far as was safe, establishing bases at suitable sites, and always looking at future explorations from those bases. These were limited aims, to start with at least, but like the grander plans of Sturt and Eyre, they would still require financial support, careful planning and suitable companions to take part in the expedition with him.

*   *   *

Financial support proved a bit problematic, as difficult in Adelaide as it had been in England. Horrocks did not have the credentials of the better-known explorers, and his small-scale plans did not hold out the possibility of grand new vistas or the returns that accompanied some of the earlier explorations in south-east Australia. Horrocks approached the Legislative Council with a modest request for 80 pounds to defray the costs of the expedition. The request was turned down. The general public were more forthcoming with their support. An association was formed in Adelaide with a Mr. George Edward Platt, the owner of a stationery supplies and library store in Hindley Street, as its secretary. The aim of the association was to support Horrocks and what was now being called his "Northern Expedition". The association proved more successful than the appeal to government and raised more than 140 pounds in just ten days.

A number of private benefactors also provided financial support, among them an Adelaide doctor named John Knott who had financially supported earlier explorations. As always, John Horrocks could rely on the almost unconditional support of his older sisters. One of them, most probably Celia, appears to have loaned him 1000 pounds towards the venture; the others lesser amounts. All sisters let him know that, when all his plans had been worked out, they wanted him to return to England with a view to re-establishing the family in Hungary.

The general planning for the expedition proceeded alongside Horrocks' other activities around Penwortham and Hope Farm, and it was not until sometime in late 1845 that he was able to begin putting all the pieces into place. One of those pieces was identifying just who his travelling companions would be. Probably the first he selected, and the man who would be his second in command, was John Henry Theakston, the mason and sculptor who had helped Arthur Horrocks build the farmhouse at Hope Farm. John approached Theakston not on the basis of that experience or because of the friendship with his brother, but on the basis that he had already proved himself on the type of expedition that Horrocks was trying to mount.

In late 1844, John Charles Darke, another young explorer who had travelled with Eyre on his 1839 expedition north to Lake Torrens, mounted an expedition of his own. His "North Western Expedition" departed Port Lincoln heading for the country to the north and west of the tip of Spencer Gulf, roughly the same area that Horrocks was interested in. Darke did not live to find out what was there. On 23 October 1844, he was speared to death by hostile Aboriginals around 150 miles north of Port Lincoln. Theakston successfully extracted the expedition from the edge of disaster and brought it back to Port Lincoln without further casualties. He had returned to work as a hotel keeper in Walkerville but agreed to join the Horrocks' expedition when the request was made.

A second man Horrocks approached also had a deep interest and involvement in the arts. His name was Samuel Thomas Gill, although he would become best known to history as S.T. Gill. Gill was almost exactly the same age as Horrocks — only two months separated their birthdays — and had already begun a career as a watercolour artist in London when his parents brought the whole family to Adelaide, arriving there in December 1839. In Adelaide, Gill opened a studio in Gawler Place in 1840, painting everything from personal likenesses to aspects of the mining operations at Burra. He had also purchased and begun using a daguerreotype camera but sold it when there appeared to be little interest in the new art of photography. He, too, accepted Horrocks' invitation to join the expedition to help document what it found.

Three others would make up the exploration party. One was Bernard Kilroy, who may have been one of the original labourers brought out from England in the first move to establish Penwortham. Kilroy would assume several responsibilities during their time away. He would be their first choice cook and would also look after the two drays that Horrocks intended to take to carry their equipment and supplies. Like all the others, though, he would also be expected to turn his hand to anything and everything necessary to make the expedition a success. Responsible for their tents and equipment — and with some duties also as regards the livestock the expedition would be taking — was a man named Garlick, probably William Garlick, the youngest son of Moses Garlick, a decorated veteran of the Napoleonic Wars who had brought his wife and three sons to Adelaide in 1838.

Finally, a young Aboriginal boy named Jimmy Moorhouse would be one of the party. He would be able to help them live off the land and, if necessary, could also help them to avoid clashed with any hostile Aboriginals they might encounter in their explorations. Jimmy would also be responsible in part for the expedition's livestock; the cattle that would pull the drays, the horses that would carry both riders and supplies, the goats Horrocks intended to purchase on the way, and Harry, the camel.

*   *   *

Sometime around the middle of 1840, the three Phillips brothers — Henry, George and Joseph — who had decided to leave their native England for South Australia, completed all the work necessary to charter the barque *Appolline* to take them and their goods and chattels from London to Adelaide. History does not tell us a lot more about the brothers, but it does provide a bit more detail about what they brought with them to South Australia. The *Appolline* visited Teneriffe in the Canary Islands quite early in the voyage, and there the Phillips' brothers purchased four camels, two males and two females. Disaster struck soon afterwards when the *Appolline* sailed into a storm. The camels had not yet been placed in their special stalls and were thrown about by the violent movements of the boat. All were injured, and three of the animals succumbed to those injuries. The fourth camel, one of the males, came ashore with the rest of the cargo when the *Appolline* anchored at Port Adelaide on 12 October 1840. It was the first camel to land in Australia.

In its edition published on 19 February 1846, the *South Australian Register* recounted this little slice of colonial history, and added, *The disconsolate survivor is now at a station in the north, his feats limited to the scaring of astonished horses who jump and fly at his approach....Their strength, docility and long endurance of drought would render them most useful to us, and they may be bought at Teneriffe for a song.*

The camel fitted into John Horrocks' plans very neatly, and he may have even modified his expedition's plans to utilise the unique attributes of the animal. Sometime after the *Register* article was published, he visited the Phillips' property and bought the camel; in exchange for the animal he gave the Phillips six cows valued at 15 pounds each. Back at Hope Farm, he named the camel Harry, in honour, perhaps of Harry Baldwin, the English conman who had duped his family. He also confirmed in his own mind how his Northern Expedition would proceed. After establishing a base camp, he would strike out into the bush using the camel. Whenever and wherever Harry blazed a suitable trail, the rest of the party would follow.

*   *   *

On 14 March 1846, in a letter to his sister, Celia, John Horrocks outlined some of what he hoped to do.

In six weeks I am going to explore to the north west of Mount Arden taking another man and a black boy. It is the only part of the colony not explored. Captain Sturt has returned after 18 months' absence and has discovered nothing but desert. We will be away four months

> *and will take the camel. I have great hopes of finding a country, and*
> *it is looked forward to with great interest by the colonists....*

He spoke of Sturt undergoing many privations and facing many dangers but added that he still looked very well, before finishing his letter.

> *We start from Mount Arden, 250 miles north of Adelaide. We know*
> *that we have 80 miles of dense scrub to get through before we reach any*
> *water. However, by God's help, we may do great good and get through*
> *all the dangers — it suits my temper as I want a more stirring life.*
>
> *I have not yet decided what I shall do when I return from my trip*
> *to the north. Should I find nothing to my liking it is probable I might*
> *return as it would be a happier life with you than leading a wandering*
> *life here with idleness my companion.*

It was typical of John Horrocks to be planning the future challenges as he prepared to face challenges that were much more immediate.

In the end, things didn't quite work out in the way Horrocks outlined in the letter to his sister. He took more companions than the two he had suggested, and it was 16 weeks before he departed. His plan to be away for four months may have remained but, to be on the safe side, he now planned to take supplies sufficient for at least five months in the bush.

*   *   *

In early July 1846, a rumour swept through Adelaide that there had been another outrage just beyond the colony's northern limits of settlement. The commonly accepted truth was that an overlanding party coming across from New South Wales had been aiming to pass through the country around the head of Spencer Gulf. That party, led by a man named Tennant, had been attacked by Aboriginals in the same area as where the

Horrocks' expedition hoped to set up its main base camp. Two shepherds had been killed outright in the attack, while 900 sheep had also been run off by the attackers. It would be several months before the story was found to be untrue but, in the meantime, the potential additional threat certainly generated additional in John Horrocks and his expedition.

The *South Australian Register* of 11 July noted: *We understand Mr Horrocks' expedition is to start today, the necessary equipment being forthcoming from private sources.*

This was a final little send-off to the expedition which headed north from Adelaide late in the morning on that winter's Saturday. The previous night, Samuel Gill had hosted a dinner for his friends, accepting their good wishes, and telling them that he was looking forward both to the forthcoming adventure and to his return to his friends afterwards.

A number of those friends no doubt congregated around the expedition as it prepared to head off the following morning. They, and the other interested spectators would have seen two drays — one large, one small — with equipment and supplies carefully stored aboard. They would have seen a number of men dressed in bushman's clothes and wearing bushman's hats, either on the drays or mounted on fine-looking horses. They may also have seen a camel and oxen pulling the drays, and maybe even a young Aboriginal boy trying to keep an eye on all the animals and all the people at the same time. And they would have seen a young man, tall and handsome and with a shock of curly brown hair, signalling the others to mount their horses or climb onto the drays before he led them off along the well-worn track to the north. He probably didn't look back; that was not John Horrocks' way.

*   *   *

The departure was more for show than anything else, of course.

Horrocks needed to both repay and reassure his backers, and a little public show in the colony's main metropolis was just one way of doing that. Horrocks led his little party back to Penwortham where they spent the next two weeks really getting ready for the expedition, packing and repacking, checking and rechecking. Horrocks set some time aside to write down his last will and testament. If he did not survive the trip, most of what he owned would be divided between his mother and older sisters, except for 500 acres of prime pastoral land on the Hutt River, which would pass to his brother, Arthur.

At noon on 29 July, Horrocks again led his small party out, this time for real. The expedition had begun.

DEPOT CREEK

That first day's travel, 12 miles northward from Penwortham on 29 July, was a gradual easing into the rhythms of an exploring expedition. Speed was not of the essence and would never become so unless the expedition's circumstances were to become dire in some way. Rather, the first few days would be like the shakedown cruise of a new warship, a chance to see how the various parts of the whole worked during a series of new and potentially stressful situations. They were still close enough to home to either return, if that were necessary, or to replace any component of the expedition, animate or inanimate, that didn't stand up to the conditions they all now faced.

The next day was also a leisurely progression in a generally northwestern direction. At some stage, Horrocks and at least one of the others rode to a property on the Hill River owned by a man named Robinson. There, they purchased 13 goats to accompany their expedition. Other explorers had taken sheep with them for food — Sturt had taken a flock of 200 on his most recent expedition — but Horrocks wanted goats rather than sheep as he believed they were better suited to the type of country he expected to encounter. He also knew that goats squealed whenever they were handled, thereby making it more difficult for Aboriginals to steal them.

The track they followed that day and the next went in a rough northwesterly direction past the little agglomerations of huts that would one day grow into the hamlet of Melrose and the village of Clare. They trekked past properties with names like Bundaleer and Bungaree, the latter the head station of the large holdings in that part of the colony owned by the Hawker brothers. They went through the same areas that John Horrocks had explored back in 1839 and 1840. Then, they were well beyond the limits of settlement; now they were part of South Australia's rural economy.

Those first few days saw some issues arise, as Horrocks had suspected they might. Late on the second day, they had some issues with one of the drays, so Horrocks asked John Theakston to take it back to Penwortham and swap it for another dray he had left at Hope Farm. He asked Theakston to also replace one of the horses and then catch up with them somewhere along the track to the Flinders Ranges. The goats also created some problems by simply wanting to wander and graze, however Jimmy Moorhouse was soon able to herd them along.

Harry the camel, though, provided the greatest challenge. No-one in the expedition had any previous experience working with camels which, given that Harry was the only camel in South Australia, was to be expected. To the men, Harry was a stubborn, stupid beast who had to be prodded into movement, and then prodded again to keep him moving. Such treatment caused the camel to become increasingly bad-tempered, even vicious at times.

The party crossed the Broughton River and headed across the Gulnare Plains on the first day of August. Harry seemed to be especially bad-tempered that day. During the morning, he seized one of the goats by its hindquarters. The goat squealed with pain and fright and was only released when Jimmy Moorhouse beat into the camel with a heavy stick. That afternoon, the camel bit William Garlick on the head as he was trying to secure its load. The attack left two deep gashes in Garlick's scalp and another tear in his cheek. Horrocks was able to repair most of the damage using poultices and sticking plaster, but the scalp wounds would take several weeks to heal completely. Frightened by the animal, the others now avoided Harry whenever possible, leaving it to Horrocks to load, unload and feed it every day.

On Sunday, 2 August, the party moved a bit further north and made a campsite alongside the Rocky River, not far from the main camp of a newly established sheep station. Named Booyoolee by its owner, Herbert Hughes, it had the distinction of being the most northerly sheep station in the colony at that time. Taking the opportunity that this presented, Horrocks sent Gill across to Hughes' camp to purchase some mutton, surmising that there would soon come a time when fresh meat was a distant memory.

The next day Horrocks led his party along the Rocky River until they reached a cattle station called Wirrabara, which was owned by a man named White. The station was already a significant operation, then carrying over 1100 head of cattle and, with White's permission, Horrocks chose to spend a rest day there to both give their horses a full days' rest and to also give John Theakston, with the new horse and dray, a chance to re-join them.

It may have been a day of rest, but the men still seemed to get quite a lot done. Jimmy Moorhouse spent the day hunting, returning in the afternoon with nothing for the pot but with a story about shooting and possibly wounding a black swan. White, the station owner, took Samuel Gill to a prominent local landmark, an enormous gum tree on a hill which provided a clear view north-west towards where Spencer Gulf lay. There, Gill spent a couple of hours making a sketch of the panorama. The forbidding bulk of the Flinders Ranges would have been a significant presence in the sketch.

Horrocks himself made the acquaintance of one of the Aboriginals who was hanging around White's homestead. Through a combination of shared words and sign language, Horrocks learned from the Aboriginal, named Kelly by someone at the station, that there was a pass through the Flinders Ranges which debouched onto the plains on the other side. Kelly offered to guide Horrocks and his party to and through the pass, an offer that Horrocks accepted. Kelly chose not to tell Horrocks that he was keen to travel in that direction because he had recently stolen a lubra from a native policeman and feared that retribution might be coming his way.

The end of the rest day featured an evening meal in which goat was the main ingredient. The men had discovered that most of the problems with the goat herd were caused by one particular goat, which was described as being unruly and belligerent. The solution to the problem was obvious and, to some, delicious as well.

John Theakston, with horses and dray, arrived during the morning of the next day, 5 August. Rather than waste any more time, the reunited party set off immediately, heading down the Rocky River to where White's Creek entered, and then up White's Creek towards the Flinders Ranges. White himself accompanied them part of the way, and they were also joined by another northern pastoralist named Malcolm Campbell who was also looking for a way through the ranges. Their camp that night would be their last in easy reach of civilization. On the morrow they would be, literally, off the map.

*   *   *

The way to the Flinders Ranges and beyond now followed Wild Dog Creek to the site of Campbell's station near the base of Mount Remarkable. There, they paused and made their final preparations. All their firearms were checked and rechecked and then loaded with musket balls rather than shot, as the latter would be ineffective against any hostile Aboriginals they encountered. The men broke camp around 10 a.m. on the morning of Saturday 8 August and, as they did so, Horrocks sent the Aboriginal Kelly back to White's station to collect a bag of clothes that he had inadvertently left behind there.

Campbell, who had opted to remain with the party as they sought a pass through the Flinders Ranges, took Samuel Gill with him to scout for likely points to gain entry into the rugged hills. The men found the plains at the foot of those ranges to be very swampy after the recent rains in the northern districts, while none of the little gullies and valleys leading into the hills held out hopes of becoming some kind of pass through them. Discouraged but not disconsolate, the men returned to the camp late in the afternoon. By way of compensation, Gill was able to shoot an emu on the return journey, providing fresh meat for dinner for them all.

The following day, the camp was moved again, further north along the base of the ranges. It was a Sunday, so no real work was attempted. One of the drays had to be unloaded to cross a creek bed, with Jimmy Moorhouse and Gill watching over the supplies before they were carried across and the dray reloaded. Bernard Kilroy, one of whose several responsibilities was that of senior cook, had another fresh emu to serve for dinner, as the dogs had also brought one down as the move between the camps was made.

While the situation was far from desperate, it was frustrating for Horrocks in that the real job of exploring could not begin until the party was into and then through the Flinders Ranges. It felt like they were wasting time, but morale remained high despite the relative lack of progress.

Late the previous day, just as they were setting up their campsite, Horrocks and Campbell had ridden further north along the foot of the ranges and believed they had spotted what may have been a pass in the distance and some way ahead. The two men rose early in the morning — it was Monday 10 August — and rode off to examine what they had spotted. The rest remained in and around the camp that day, except for Samuel Gill. The campsite was near an abutment rising from the plain, a small extension of the ranges that they had called Stoney Point. Carrying his sketching materials in a valise, Gill climbed to the top of the abutment, where he drew two sketches of the countryside around their campsite.

Horrocks and Campbell returned to the campsite around 4 p.m., bringing a mix of good and bad news. The good news was that the pass they had spotted the previous evening did indeed lead into the heart of the ranges where there were other valleys they could follow down to the plains beyond. The bad news was that the route was very narrow in parts and was not suited to their drays. However, they did not feel that any of the problems they might face were insurmountable, and Horrocks proposed striking out for the pass and beyond as soon as they broke camp the following morning.

The entire party set out with high hopes the next day. The pass that Horrocks and Campbell had scouted was a relatively wide valley that rose and narrowed as it climbed towards the high point of the ranges. There were many small side valleys off it. In times of rain, each of these would have contained rivulets which combined to form a substantial creek flowing down the main valley. That creek was dry now, but its uneven surface of sand and rocks, and the raised banks of the creek bed, meandered up and down the valley. The creek's various twists and turns meant that it would have to be crossed several times if the drays were to stick to relatively level ground. Unfortunately, disaster struck as they attempted their very first creek bed crossing.

Both drays were unloaded to make the crossing easier, but the first to attempt it broke the near arm of one of its axles trying to climb out of the creek bed. Horrocks called an immediate halt and held a brief discussion with the others. He was obviously upset that this had happened just as they began their ascent and told the others that it was a setback rather than a disaster. They would make this spot a campsite and unload the second dray there. They would attach horses to the second dray, which

Kilroy would take back to White's station to see if they could procure yet another axle. The tents were then pitched in the most convenient places, and the men settled in at their new campsite.

Once Kilroy had departed, Horrocks and John Theakston started to walk further up the valley and into the uplands to see if there was anything that could be done immediately to make progress easier when they eventually resumed the expedition. It was well and truly dark by the time they returned and reported to the others that the way ahead appeared to be relatively free of impediments.

Discussions around the campfire continued well into the night. Horrocks again discussed with Gill the option of them riding well ahead of the main body to examine the country around the head of Spencer Gulf, but both felt that dividing the expedition offered no advantages in their current circumstances. Instead, they would use their horses and camel to move their equipment and supplies through the ranges, depositing them on the other side before returning for the empty drays. Other options could be canvassed once they had crossed the ranges.

They rested and planned for most of the following day. Samuel Gill spent the morning reworking some of the sketches he had previously drawn while John Theakston polished and checked his navigational instruments preparatory to taking measurements of the sun at noon. During the afternoon, Horrocks walked up the valley and climbed to the summit of one of the hills which flanked it. The views were as extensive as they were unimpressive, and Gill noted in his diary: *"Rocky; grey and red stone. North-west prospect very cheerless. One hill distant, 100 miles; fires about 30 miles off"*.

Despite this, Horrocks was impressed by the distances he could see in all directions and recommended the climb to the others.

That day, they had begun to move the supplies and equipment in stages up the valley, a process they would continue over the next several days. It was not all work, and several availed themselves of the opportunity to have a good look around. The day after Horrocks had climbed to the top of the hill that offered panoramic views of their surrounds, Gill and Jimmy Moorhouse made the same ascent. Gill wanted to make some sketches of that view and thought Jimmy would be a good companion who could also help carry his easel and pencils. Gill also found the climb up rough and stony ground a lot more difficult than he had expected, and admitted to being 'spent' by the time he returned to camp at 4 p.m.

By the end of the week, most of the supplies had been relocated to points near the top of the valley, and the men had little to do beyond waiting for Bernard Kilroy to return with horses, dray and, hopefully, another axle. On Friday, 14 August, John Theakston and Jimmy Moorhouse went out hunting for fresh meat. They shot a young female kangaroo which Jimmy carried on his shoulders back to their campsite. It was cleaned and cooked for that night's dinner, and the travellers were very surprised when Jimmy, although hungry, refused to eat any of it.

When asked why, Jimmy explained that, in his tribe, the 'priests' or holy men had told all the young men that 'God', or the higher powers above man, had determined that all delicacies, like the flesh of young female kangaroos, had been especially reserved for the elders of the tribe. Should a young man such as Jimmy eat any of those delicacies, they would die immediately.

Samuel Gill finally lost patience with the leading goat, a large white male, the following day. It had turned nasty, almost as if it were returning to a wild and native state, and its behaviour was starting to impact on that of the other goats. Tracking it down and then throwing it to the ground, Gill was able to hobble its front legs, meaning it would not stray too far from camp again. Gill thought it was a job well done.

During that Saturday afternoon, Bernard Kilroy arrived back from White's station, bringing with him a pair of axle arms for the crippled dray. Almost as soon as he had come to a halt, Horrocks and Theakston were at work on the dray. They first drove the box from the centre of the affected wheel and put in another in which they would seat one end of the new axle arm. When that arm was fitted, and the wheel attached, the dray was fully operational and almost as good as new.

Kelly and his lubra had both travelled back and returned with Kilroy, and it was decided that they could further assist the party. Malcolm Campbell had returned to his own property after he and Horrocks had found the pass through the ranges, leaving behind a number of tools he thought they might need to make the pass navigable. Some of these were no longer required and could be returned to him. Samuel Gill had also completed a detailed sketch of White's station, and it was thought that Kelly could take all of those things back with him.

By the end of the day, the explorers were all very positive, looking forward to a move early on Monday morning after resting for most of the Sabbath, with the belief that getting over "this fearful range" was now almost within their grasp.

*   *   *

Rather than waste an expedition day, Horrocks and Theakston spent Sunday afternoon supervising the careful loading of the drays and pack animals, making adjustments to each until the best distribution of what remained in their camp was achieved. Horrocks' plans for using Kelly had also changed, and he now decided to take the Aboriginal with them as they descended down to the plains on the far side of the ranges. They would travel across to the head of the Gulf, examine the countryside there, and prepare reports and letters for their families and for their backers in Adelaide. Kelly could carry these back to White's station, and they could be forwarded on from there. It was an idea which obviously held no attraction for Kelly, who at some stage during the night, took his lubra and simply disappeared. The general belief was that he had run away because the party was about to enter the lubra's tribal territory where she would probably be taken away from him.

The party, less Kelly and the lubra, moved out before daybreak on Monday morning. On their first trip they took the heavy dray, the pack-horses, the camel and the goats to a relatively flat and sheltered spot they had previously reconnoitred near the top of the pass. They unhitched the bullock from the dray and led them back down to their campsite, hitched them to the lighter dray, and again ascended the pass. The whole operation went like clockwork and was completed without any mishap.

Their good fortune did not continue during the descent. By trial and error, Horrocks had determined that the camel could carry up to around 350 pounds' weight without any seeming discomfort. He loaded Harry with probably a bit less than that for the descent, but Harry was now in a black mood. Among the load he was expected to carry down the hill were several bags of flour that Horrocks had attached to his pack saddle. For some reason, these seemed to annoy the camel, who firstly bit at his lead rope as Horrocks guided him down the main gully, and then attacked the wheat bags themselves. He bit through one, scattering its contents, and then bolted past Horrocks down the gully.

As he ran, most of the wheat bags bounced off his pack, splitting open when they hit the ground. Other items were similarly disposed of. Horrocks eventually found Harry standing quietly in one of the side gullies, and he gave no trouble as he was led back to the resting place at the top of the pass. There, he was reloaded with items from the heavy dray. In three uneventful trips, Harry carried most of the dray's load down to a site where the gully opened up with the western plains just a short trip below.

The two drays proved to be even more troublesome than the camel on the descent. The horses, rather than the bullocks, were hitched to them as the men believed that they would be nimbler. In the end, it probably didn't make all that much difference. The creek bed that meandered down the valley on that side of the range had to be crossed over several times to make the best use of the relatively flat ground which bordered it. On one crossing, the heavy dray tipped over as it was entering the creek bed. Almost alongside it, the second dray also tipped as the horses tried to pull it up and out of the creek bed. It took the men quite a while to right the wagons, and it was approaching dusk when they finished. Horrocks led them all down to where the supplies had been dumped, and they made a small campsite there. A quick meal and they collapsed, exhausted, into their sleeping rolls.

*   *   *

The next morning, the descent continued. Horrocks took the camel up to where the drays had capsized, and in several trips brought down everything that had either been left at the top of the pass or where the drays had tipped. While he was doing this, the other men were working with shovels to level out the banks of the creek where all the trouble had occurred. Doing so took three hours of hard work, but they finished it off well enough for the horses to be able to pull the drays across and out of the creek bed and down to the camp they had set up above where the gully met the plain.

Horrocks decreed that they had done enough for one day. Before their evening meal, the men all walked the short distance to the point where the plains commenced and then a short distance out onto them. They expressed the belief that the worst of the country was now behind them while Horrocks said that an hour's travel, or maybe a bit more, the next day should bring them to Depot Creek and its supply of fresh water.

Of course, it did not turn out to be as simple as that. There was further work necessary on the creek bed near the bottom of the gully to ensure

129

that the earlier accidents were not repeated. One of the men also found what appeared to be a permanent water pool not all that far from where they had camped and Horrocks made the decision that all their livestock would be watered, and their water casks refilled, before they headed out onto the plains. All this took time, and it was well into the afternoon before they formed up and moved out onto the plains. This in turn meant that they did not travel far, three miles or so, before Horrocks called a halt and they set up a new campsite. Looking back, the large gully they had ascended was clearly visible, picked out by the setting sun. It would be known as Horrocks' Pass, a decision made by Horrocks himself, but one with which they all concurred.

*   *   *

The party moved out again at half past nine the next morning — it was now Thursday 26 August — and began to trek across what Horrocks would describe as "a most desolate plain". He also believed the party was now entering the country where Tennant's party had been attacked and the two shepherds killed, so he advised everyone to keep an eye out for possible hostile natives. After a trek of what Theakston estimated to have been 24 miles, Horrocks called a halt on the banks of what would have been a large creek had there been any water in it. He told the others he believed that they were now very close to Depot Creek.

Earlier in the day, Gill had shot a large kangaroo, and as it was being prepared for dinner, he decided to ride up the dry creek bed to look for water holes, or anything else of interest. He had not gone very far when he came across an old, and very startled, Aboriginal man. Using a mixture of basic hand gestures and words that Jimmy Moorhouse had taught him, Gill indicated that he was looking for water, and believed that the old man indicated that he had just ridden straight past a waterhole or soak. Gill retraced his steps, but could find no trace of water, so he returned to the campsite to inform the others of what had happened.

The encounter intrigued Horrocks, who said he would like to speak to the old Aboriginal. On horseback, they returned to where Gill had encountered the old man. He was no longer there, but Gill spotted him, some distance away and out on the plain. He was running in the direction of Depot Creek and, moreover, he was not alone. Trotting alongside him were four, much younger Aboriginal.

The explorers remained in their camp overnight, their sleep somewhat disturbed by the horses who were becoming increasingly desperate for water. The men could hear them, snorting and shuffling around. In the morning, they found that the horses had even gone so far as licking and nibbling the plugs on the water casks. They had then wandered off in the general direction of the previous campsite, where they knew there was water nearby. They were easy to spot using the telescope, and easily caught when approached.

The party broke camp and headed for Depot Creek at 9.30 a.m. It was not a difficult journey and was made easier by simply following the tracks made by Eyre's party some six years earlier. All up, it took just 90 minutes to arrive at the campsite established by Eyre and Darke and just a little bit longer to find the spring that Eyre's party had used. A little digging provided good water and the horses, now waterless for 36 hours, were the first to be watered there. They were followed by the cattle with the goats last of all. The area also had a plentiful supply of what Horrocks called oaten grass, which all the animals ate; it was easy to see why Eyre had chosen the site for his depot.

Part of that afternoon was devoted to talking through what the next moves would be. Horrocks said that the next day, he and Theakston would ride to the head of the Gulf to see whether there were any crossing points through the swamps that others had found there and, if so, to see whether they could find a suitable site for another depot on the other side of the swamps. If not, they would begin to strike out from Depot Creek towards the tableland which could be seen faintly in the distance to the north-west.

The day ended with a feast, of sorts. The troublesome white goat, which managed to upset the other goats even while hobbled, was killed and cooked by Bernard Kilroy, who also saved and cleaned the goat's hide at Horrocks' direction. His plan was to fashion the hide into one or two water bags. Those bags, he explained, would be carried by the camel with far less difficulty than one of the water casks, for instance. He added that, where they were going, that water might well mean the difference between life and death.

A Beautiful, Fatal Bird

The push to the north-west began in earnest on Friday 22 August when John Horrocks and Samuel Gill set off to examine some small, flat-topped hills which lay about 16 miles away in that direction. They set off, armed and on horseback, shortly after breakfast and soon found that the country beyond Depot Creek was no different to that they had crossed to reach Depot Creek: low scrub, patchy grass and everywhere the tracks of kangaroos, emus and wallabies.

En route to the low hills, the men crossed several small dry creek beds, and at length came to a small lake, which was also dry. They crossed this at its neck, where the main water channel would enter it during heavy rains, and found that the sand there was exceptionally soft and treacherous in parts. They also found that the terrain changed on the far side of the lake. There, they had to cross a succession of low sand ridges rather than sand hills, all covered with a small, dry and very dusty shrub. Beyond that, the natural surface and vegetation of the plain continued as the men rode steadily north-west, keeping an eye out for either forage or water, but without success.

As the two horsemen approached the base of the largest of the flat-topped hills, they spotted two Aboriginals standing on a large patch of flat land covered by the dusty scrub. Horrocks and Gill had approached to within 400 yards of the couple before they were spotted but, when

133

they were, both Aboriginals started to run away from them. Urging their horses into a canter, the explorers took off after the fleeing figures and were soon close enough to see that they were chasing a woman and a small child, both of whom were clearly apprehensive of the men and more so of the horses.

Reining in their horses in front of the frightened Aboriginal, both Horrocks and Gill used sign language and gestures to indicate that they were looking for water and asked the woman to show them where it could be found. When the woman turned and moved off, they followed her, riding through the scrub for around two miles until they came upon three more Aboriginal children, who fled at their approach. The woman looked as though she wanted to run off after them but, after a brief pause, she continued on in the direction she had been travelling. In a relatively short space, certainly not more than 800 yards, they found two Aboriginal men and another child.

The two men simply stood and stared at the Europeans for a moment and then started to walk towards them. As they did so, they put down the baskets they had both been carrying and picked up spears which had been lying on the ground nearby. When they were drawing close, Gill and Horrocks both motioned for the men to sit down, which they did. They dismounted and spoke to the two Aboriginal, again making signs for water.

By now, the woman and child had both disappeared somewhere in the bush, while the men spoke to Horrocks and Gill in a loud and an aggressive manner. For several minutes, neither of the Aboriginal men showed any inclination to take them to water or to even move in any direction. The Europeans tried a variety of tactics, walking over to and laughing with the Aboriginal, patting them on the back, and generally acting in what they believed was an exceedingly friendly manner. After a while, the younger of the two men stood up and began to move off. The older man followed him but was obviously reluctant to do so.

The water they had been seeking was just 30 yards away. It was in the form of a large puddle rather than a waterhole. A few inches of muddy rainwater that appeared to have drained down from the hills and was now drying up. The horses lapped it up. The Aboriginal seemed to indicate that there were waterholes in three other directions, but again showed no inclination to take the Europeans to any of them. Rather, they just stood up and watched Horrocks and Gill; they, too, were obviously scared of the European's horses.

Horrocks then gave both the men some tobacco leaf, but it appeared to both he and Gill that they simply ate the leaf. To show them what he meant, Horrocks took another piece of tobacco, crushed it into the bowl of his pipe, and lit the pipe with his burning glass; both the Aboriginals seemed monumentally disinterested in this demonstration. In fact, both men appeared to be increasingly ill at ease. The older man started to draw back from the group, so Horrocks and Gill took their guns and pistols from their holsters, but again without exciting any interest from the Aboriginal.

The younger Aboriginal, who had a piece of red cloth tied around his head, seemed to understand the word knife but, like his older companion he, too, started to back away from the Europeans. By then, the older man was some yards distant and was both signalling and calling out loudly, presumably threatening Horrocks and Gill while calling the young man back. At this point, Horrocks fired one barrel of his gun into the air, but even that failed to generate any response from the Aboriginal.

Considering they could do no more, Gill and Horrocks both had a drink, watered their horses again, and set off back towards the southern end of the flat-topped hills they had been making for. It was a distance of about two miles and, once there, they dismounted and tied their horses together. They then climbed up the side of the hill, quite a difficult task as it was both steep and exceptionally stony.

At the top of the hill, the men used the telescope to examine the country even further out towards the north-west, as that was still where Horrocks intended to explore. To Gill, the country appeared to be a desert, *"one immense space of dry, sandy country with a low, crisp scrub without the slightest sign of grass or probability of water."* Gill sketched what he could see from that vantage point while he and Horrocks discussed aloud and at length whether or not it would be possible to cross the land that lay ahead. When Gill had finished his sketch, they returned to their horses and rode back to the waterhole, where they knew there was also some grass for the horses.

Just as they reined in at the waterhole, Gill realised that he had some-how mislaid a quart pot and his compass. The two men retraced their short ride but could find no trace of either.

The Aboriginals they had spoken to earlier had by now moved well away from the waterhole and could be seen further away at the base of a low hill. To both Horrocks and Gill, they seemed to be restless rather than threatening. The men watered their horses from what was now a red brick dust coloured bog and let them graze awhile on the oaten grass before remounting and turning back in the direction of Depot Creek. They had only travelled a short distance, a couple of hundred yards at most, when they were confronted by a lone Aboriginal man carrying a fire stick. He waved the stick at them both while shouting out what both men took to be threats against them.

They then spotted, on a small hill and just 100 yards away, a small group of Aboriginals who were also shouting at them. This group were all carrying spears, and when they started running down the hill towards where Horrocks and Gill sat astride their horses, the two men took up their guns and fired, Horrocks discharging both barrels of his shot gun. The men deliberately fired short, and the three musket balls kicked up little puffs of dust where they struck.

The Aboriginals stopped at this and looked around, apparently uncertain about what had just happened. They looked closely at the ground where the musket balls had hit and moved away from it. Horrocks and Gill both reloaded their guns and then rode slowly towards the Aboriginal, who retreated back to the top of the hill, from where they yelled and laughed down at the Europeans. The horsemen stopped some 80 yards short of the hill and fired in front of the Aboriginals again, causing them to again retreat, this time back over the crest of the hill.

By now, it was quite late in the afternoon, and Horrocks in particular wanted to get clear of the area. He led the way, and the two men cantered through the scrub to a point half a dozen miles away from the hills in the direction of Depot Creek. There they stopped and camped for the night.

*   *   *

The next morning, Horrocks and Gill rose at dawn and smoked their pipes before mounting their horses and continuing on. It was still early when they set out across the plains and they recrossed the empty creek beds before they arrived back at Depot Creek around 10 a.m. in the morning. The first thing they did was eat a real breakfast. They then looked to the horses after what Gill estimated had been a 50-mile ride with very little food and only just enough water. The horses were hobbled and turned loose to graze while Horrocks and Gill had a bath, of sorts, at the spring.

During the remainder of that day, Horrocks had a number of discussions with the other members of the party and, as a result, came to a decision about what they would attempt next. In line with what he had originally planned, they would continue to use Depot Creek as a base to push further into what seemed to be the interior deserts of the colony and the continent. The next reconnaissance inland would be in the direction of a large tableland or rising country that had been noted, but not explored, by the Eyre and Darke expedition six years earlier. He estimated that the feature was approximately 80 miles distant from their current base and, once there, he would decide on what next to do, where next to go.

On this reconnaissance he would be accompanied by two of the party — Gill and Bernard Kilroy — while John Theakston would remain in charge of the base at Depot Creek. Horrocks estimated that the reconnaissance would take two weeks, but his little party would take rations sufficient for three. The men would travel on foot with their equipment and supplies being carried by the camel. Horrocks would also be looking for a permanent water supply, such as they had at Depot Creek and, if such a spot was found, he would return and they would use the drays to carry everything to what would become their new base of operations.

That day was Sunday 23 August. There was still a bit to do, but Horrocks said that he hoped to depart around the end of the week.

*   *   *

With the start of a new week, and with the first major reconnaissance in the offing, a number of significant activities started. The first was the relocation of their base camp further up Depot Creek from Eyre's original site. For all the comfort and familiarity of that site, it was still a hundred yards or more from the spring, which was their only source of fresh water; a relatively short trip but one that was becoming increasingly tiresome. The move occupied most of the first morning and was completed to Horrocks' satisfaction by early afternoon.

Once he had established just what the main issues to be addressed before they departed were, he made a brief site inspection, spoke to the men and then, restless as usual, he continued his own exploration of the areas around their campsite, this time heading down the Depot Creek bed and away from the others. When he returned several hours later, he told the others that he had found several tobacco plants growing some distance downstream and showed them an example of leaf he had picked. They could only speculate on how the plants came to be there.

After the new campsite was completed, and while Horrocks was off exploring on his own, the others filled in the time in their own ways. Gill was, as usual, working on his various sketches while Theakston cleaned and checked his navigational instruments. Others checked on the animals and the equipment, loaded cartridges for their various guns, prepared meals and the like.

The next morning, John Theakston and Jimmy Moorhouse took the dogs and went out hunting. Fresh meat was always welcome in the camp and, with the northern reconnaissance about to commence, it might be possible to salt or jerk some meat for them to take as ration supplements as well. Theakston's hunting party flushed out two large kangaroos and two adult emus from the scrub, but they were unable to catch any of them as the dogs proved incapable of slowing them, let alone bringing them down. For Theakston, the failure reinforced his belief that while their greyhounds were certainly fast enough to keep up with such prey, they lacked both the weight and the strength to drag them down.

It was also another day of preparation for the expedition north, for the sorting of stores and discussions about what to take and what to leave behind. Gill finally finished a number of the sketches he had begun as they crossed the Flinders Ranges, and the others continued their work to bring this, their main base, into the most appropriate configuration they could. As their group would split in half during the expedition, certain accommodations would need to be made.

Most of the stores and equipment, for instance, had simply been left on one or other of the drays, covered by a tarpaulin and accessed when they were needed. The departure of Horrocks, Gill and Kilroy meant that one large tent would become vacant while another would have some extra space available. The men decided that the large tent would therefore be used to store everything that was currently on the drays. Not only would that keep those stores and equipment well out of the elements, it would mean they were a lot more secure should Aboriginals decide to visit the camp.

Both the elements and the Aboriginals were discussed at length that week as the weather was changing and changing quite dramatically. Daytime temperatures were now on the hot side of warm, with early hints of the summer to come. With the heat came the flies, just to add something else to the discomfort of humans and animals alike. Those flies and that heat also presumably discomfited the local Aboriginal, although that was just a guess as the Europeans had not seen any since Horrocks' and Gill's encounter at the little hills to the north-west. They were all convinced that there were Aboriginals somewhere in the neighbourhood; they also suspected that they were now deliberately avoiding the explorers' camp.

John Horrocks also used the time to work with the camel, testing its capacity and endurance. After several short excursions carrying various loads and load configurations, he was convinced that Harry could easily travel 25 miles a day carrying a load of 350 pounds' weight, with a minimum of food and water, and with the prickly desert bushes providing all the nourishment he required. He was also convinced that he had mastered the animal, finding it now quite easy to handle. It would both kneel and rise at his command, and its dark moods seemed to be occurring less frequently. He, too, was disappointed with the dogs though. On Wednesday, Jimmy Moorhouse took him out hunting, and they spotted an emu. The dogs went after it but, like the others, it too was able to escape.

Preparations for the reconnaissance were finalised on the Thursday, 27 August. In the morning, Horrocks and Theakston rode back to the Flinders Ranges and climbed to a high point there — probably Mount

Arden — and from there took bearings on the large plateau they now estimated to be some 100 miles north-west from where they were. Back at the Depot Creek base, Theakston took a reading of the sun at midday, and then undertook the calculations that would give Horrocks and his party a clear and accurate course to follow. When they departed, they would need to follow a compass bearing of 32 degrees north of west.

By the time all this had been completed, Horrocks felt that it was too late to depart that day and announced that his party would leave as early as possible the next morning. The rest of the day was spent in final preparations for that departure. Experience had taught Horrocks that the camel would bridle at carrying anything he considered too weighty. Using a combination of guesswork and trial and error, Horrocks finally came up with a composite load of utensils and supplies for Harry to carry; he estimated their total weight to be 356 pounds.

Samuel Gill was facing similar problems. Part of his role was to provide a pictorial record of the expedition, and paper, pens, pencils and brushes were the tools he used to do this. He had brought plenty with him but needed to take only the essentials on this trip. It was tricky, but when all the decisions had been made, he packed everything carefully into a valise. Gill had also hoped to take his pony; he didn't really enjoy walking, and the pony could also have shared part of the load, but that idea was vetoed as there was no guarantee that they would find either fresh water or forage as they travelled.

Eventually, everything was more or less sorted out, it was dusk, and the new day was almost upon them.

*   *   *

Friday 28 August 1846 dawned wet and windy. They were hardly ideal conditions to start the expedition, but they were, in many ways, better than the previous few days with the excessive early season heat and interminable swarms of flies. The drabness of the day also seemed to reduce the imperative to be up and on the way early, and it was a quarter past ten before they departed Depot Creek.

Nor did Horrocks push hard that day. When they completed the loading of the camel that morning, they had put on what he had estimated to be three weeks' worth of rations and ten gallons of fresh water. Easy travelling on days like this meant that what they had brought might last even longer than he had estimated. They walked until dusk, at which time Horrocks guessed that they had covered around ten miles. Most of it had been through level scrub, although the last four miles had been across red sand hills covered by the same oaten grass that they had found at Depot Creek.

The place they camped that first night was alongside one of the dry creek beds that criss-crossed the area. Horrocks believed that most of them, when full, actually drained water from Lake Torrens into Spencer Gulf, and gave this one the name, Salty Creek. As the wet weather continued into the night, the men chose not to mount an overnight watch to protect against possible hostile Aboriginal.

The explorers were up and moving by half past eight the next morning and would travel what Horrocks estimated to be 15 miles that day. The first eight miles of the day's trek had been on those same red sand hills and oaten grass, which had then given way to the now familiar plain covered with the short grey-green shrubs. There were also stony patches and what the explorers termed salsolaceous plants. At the end of the day, they were back at the low, flat-topped hills that Horrocks and Gill had visited the previous week.

It had been a dismal day's travelling, the scenery dreary and the weather cool with the occasional rain shower washing over them. Perhaps it was that dreariness that prompted Horrocks to give the little flat-topped hills within which they set up camp the rather grandiose title of the Table Ranges and the little gully they camped in the name, Stoney Pass. With little else to do, the men sat and talked well into the evening, staying up until the moon set.

The men cleared the Table Ranges early the next morning and continued on through country that alternated between the light scrub they were now used to and many sandy ridges that were quite heavily covered by the same scrub. At no time did they find either permanent water or suitable pasturage in either of those two environments. Nor did they see any other human beings, although they crossed the relatively fresh tracks of several Aboriginal.

As they advanced further out onto the plains, they did find several quite large puddles of rainwater, sufficient to both water the camel and replenish the small water casks that he carried, the proposed goat skin containers having failed to materialise.

The party had moved a little bit faster that day, and when Horrocks called a halt with dusk starting to descend, he estimated that they had travelled 16 miles from the previous night's campsite. It would have been more, he opined, but moving up and down the sand hills had impacted on the distance they were able to travel. The weather had remained cool, with occasional showers, and their campsite that night was in the middle of the scrub without any protection from the weather. Nor was there any protection from hostile Aboriginal. Knowing that they were in an area familiar to Aboriginal, that night they all took turns to act as guards, Samuel Gill taking the first shift.

The men moved on from their makeshift camp in the scrub at a quarter to nine the next morning, having survived the night without any alarms or excursions. Early that day, they continued trekking through the same sort of terrain and vegetation to that they had camped in but, after a time, they noticed that the size of the straggly scrub seemed to be increasing.

They were still able to navigate and travel without difficulty, and the scrub eventually gave way to a sterile, stony plain. Once they had crossed that plain, they had a clear view of their objective, the table land ahead rising out of the grey-green scrub that had begun again at the other side of the three-mile-wide gibber plain.

The party halted for an hour around the middle of the day. The bad weather of the previous days had blown over, and they found it increasingly hot and tiresome work walking under a fierce sun. The halt was to rest themselves and the camel, and to also reward him by walking around where they had stopped and collecting the kinds of plants they had seen him grazing on previously. After the break, they continued walking across the plains until Horrocks called a halt at 6 p.m., primarily because the camel seemed quite fatigued by then.

In their discussions after dinner, all three expressed the hope that the next day they would find permanent water, as the hot day had led to a greater consumption than they had expected. The sky at dusk had also suggested the possibility of overnight showers so, just in case, they dug several holes in the sand near their tent and lined the holes with their oilskin capes to collect any rain which fell.

*   *   *

The men were all up and about early the next morning, a Tuesday, the first day of September and therefore the first day of the southern spring. They were walking by 8.30 and continued without a break until midday, covering more than six miles in that time. They stopped because they came upon a large saltwater lake or, rather, a large salt pan that would become a lake when it was full. Now, it was a large expanse of relatively flat ground comprising the colours of the desert — ochre reds and browns — interspersed with patches of almost blindingly white salt and the darker hues of dirt and clay; they could all see the sparkle of water out in the middle of the lakebed. Horrocks, who said he believed the lake to be about ten miles long and probably five wide, also suggested they walk out to where the water sat.

The three men all walked across the speckled land to the water's edge, quite a distance out from its former shoreline, and each scooped up a handful of the clear liquid to try; all found it exceedingly salty. Looking around, they could see that they were in a shallow depression which drained the country for a considerable distance around them. After clearing his throat and giving a suitable pause, Horrocks announced that he was going to name this lake, Lake Gill, after his fellow explorer, friend and the colony's foremost artist, Samuel Gill.

After handshakes all around, Horrocks then pointed out their next objective, the base of the tablelands they had come to explore. He also spotted a small rise between where they were and the tableland and suggested that was where they would stay that night as the tableland appeared to be around 25 miles from where they stood. To get there, they would need to return to where the camel had been tethered and then proceed along the eastern shoreline of the lake to its northernmost extremity before striking out across the plain again for the rise he could see from where they stood. When they returned to the lake's edge, Gill asked if it would be possible to draw a sketch of the lake named in his honour from the point where they had intercepted it.

In giving his assent, Horrocks also pointed out that they would take a break and eat there as well. They would rest for a while during the heat of the day and resume when the sun had dropped a bit further towards the horizon. They would camp to the north of the lake that night and move on to the tablelands the next day.

They resumed walking around the middle of the afternoon. About an hour later, as they were rounding the northern end of the lake, Bernard

Kilroy, who was walking 50 yards ahead of the others, suddenly stopped and held up his hand.

"*What is it?*" Horrocks called out.

"*A beautiful bird,*" Kilroy replied in a voice the others strained to hear. "*You should shoot it for the collection; it really is beautiful,*" Kilroy said, never taking his eyes off a spot in the scrub a short distance ahead.

This created an immediate problem, but one that Horrocks knew was not insurmountable. His shotgun was hanging from loops attached to the camel's pack saddle and it was already loaded. Unfortunately, it was loaded with the wrong ammunition. The cartridge in one barrel contained a musket ball and the cartridge in the other barrel contained several slightly smaller balls known as slugs; both had been loaded with the expectation that if the gun was fired, it would be aimed at something much larger than a small bird, a kangaroo perhaps, or even a human being should they be attacked by hostile Aboriginal. In normal circumstances, he could have replaced the shot in one of the barrels by the simple expedients of firing the gun. He could not do so now because firing a shot would doubtless scare the bird away. Nor could he shoot the bird with either of the cartridges as a direct hit would simply reduce the beautiful bird to a pile of bloodstained feathers.

Speaking rapidly to Gill, Horrocks explained what he wanted to do. Both of them would walk back to Harry, who had stopped behind them when the two men had stopped. Horrocks would have the camel kneel and, when it did, he would take his gun's ramrod from its sheath below the barrels and with it remove the wad which covered the slugs in the cartridge in the gun's right barrel. While he was doing this, Gill should locate the shot belt, also attached to the camel's pack saddle, and take from the relevant pouch in that belt a small charge of bird shot. When both operations were complete, Horrocks would remove the shotgun from the loops, tip it over so the slugs fell out, then replace them with the bird shot and prepare to shoot the bird. Gill nodded his understanding.

It started out well — Harry knelt at Horrocks' command — but then it all went horribly wrong. Gill and Horrocks were both on the near side of the camel, Horrocks hurriedly removing the ramrod and pushing it hard into the right barrel of the shotgun and Gill searching for the right pocket in the shot belt. Neither noticed that the pack saddle had shifted slightly when the camel knelt and that part of it had forced the right hammer back and was now holding it back under a certain amount of pressure. The camel suddenly lurched, Gill would later suspect that it had settled on a sharp stone, the saddle moved again, releasing the hammer which struck the cartridge. The gun exploded in Horrocks' face as the cartridge he was manipulating was fired.

In less time than it takes to blink an eye, Horrocks was critically injured and the explorers' world was turned upside down. The ramrod sliced through the middle finger of Horrocks' right hand, all but severing the finger. The main charge of slugs struck Horrocks' face at an angle; had they hit squarely he would have been dead in an instant. Even the glancing blow did a horrible amount of damage. It struck the left lower side of Horrocks' face breaking his lower jaw and smashing most of the teeth, upper and lower, on that side. It also removed most of the muscle and skin from that part of his face. He fell back, unconscious, and bleeding profusely from both wounds.

After an initial paralysis from shock at what had happened, both Gill and Kilroy sprang into action. They turned the wounded man over onto his good side, made a quick examination of the wounds, and set to work to do what they could to save the man's life. The first thing to do was to stop the bleeding. Two-thirds of Horrocks' right middle finger was attached to his hand by a small sliver of skin; they cut through this with a knife and bound the stump tightly with a handkerchief. They repeated most of the process on the gaping facial wound. Fortunately, they had a medicine chest of sorts. Fearing spear wounds in any possible clash with Aboriginal, they had disinfectant, which they put on the wound before covering it with a clean handkerchief and holding the whole thing in place with a bandage.

All this done, and Horrocks still unconscious, they began to look a bit further ahead. Firstly, they set up the tent alongside the spot where the accident had occurred and then carried Horrocks inside and laid him down on the bed they had prepared for him. After a brief discussion, it was agreed that Gill would remain with Horrocks while Kilroy returned to Depot Creek as quickly as he could. He would there apprise Theakston of the accident before returning with a dray to carry the wounded man. They estimated that Kilroy would have to travel a minimum of 60 miles through rough country. By now, they had only five gallons of fresh water remaining. Kilroy took a small portion of that, a few biscuits as well and, after adjusting his compass, disappeared into the gathering gloom.

Not long after Kilroy departed, Gill was sitting inside the tent with Horrocks when the explorer regained consciousness. Although he was in great pain, Horrocks was able to speak, albeit with great difficulty and in a way that was sometimes hard to understand. Gill was somewhat relieved by this, as he feared that Horrocks' brain might have been affected by what his body had suffered. He slipped into and out of consciousness throughout the night, while Gill was not prepared to let himself fall asleep. It was, he would later write, *"a wretched night"*.

Coming Home

Bernard Kilroy had 65 miles to cover to reach Depot Creek, but that was 65 miles of a straight line drawn on a map. Kilroy had a lot more than that to travel. There were sand ridges and sand hills to climb up and down, lakes and lake beds to go around and thick patches of scrub to skirt. In bright sunlight, and with a little luck, he could pick out the tracks their party had made on the outward journey, but there were other times, too, at the gibber plain for instance, when they had simply left no discernible tracks. When that occurred, and it did several times, he could trust his compass, cast about for their tracks, or try his luck. He did all three at times.

At 9 p.m. on 2 September, 27 hours after he had left the stricken Horrocks and Gill, Kilroy stumbled into the base camp at Depot Creek. In those 27 hours, he guessed that he had covered around 100 miles of desert and consumed no more than a pint of water and a couple of biscuits while doing so. It was a tremendous feat of human endurance.

*　　*　　*

At the tent back where Kilroy had left Horrocks in the care of Samuel Gill, the artist felt that Horrocks seemed just a little bit better the morning after the terrible accident. He had slept fitfully during the night, with

Gill a constant presence beside him. Gill had replaced the original face bandage with a poultice, and this gave Horrocks' swollen features an even more grotesque appearance. The injury, and the accompanying shock, meant that Horrocks was not able to eat anything solid and had struggled to drink as well. Gill's solution had been to keep Horrocks' lips moistened during the night and to encourage him to swallow a little cold water by squeezing it into drops from the end of a towel dipped in fresh water.

When he was certain that Horrocks was fully awake, he repeated the process using lukewarm tea instead of cold water. Tea, he thought, would be a source of some nourishment and, being warm, would be less likely to aggravate any of the shocking injuries that Horrocks' mouth and cheek had suffered. Then, as Horrocks lay back on his bed, Gill bathed his forehead and face in warm water too. He spoke aloud as well, believing that Horrocks could hear and understand everything he said. He spoke of what had happened, and how Kilroy had immediately left to fetch help and how he would soon return. He spoke, too, of what would happen then, the return to the settled districts and Penwortham, and perhaps beyond that to Adelaide. He spoke until he noticed that Horrocks had again drifted off to sleep.

During the day, Gill managed to almost convince himself that Horrocks was visibly improving, slowly but surely taking the first step on the long road to recovery. He slept fitfully during the day but would take either water or tea when he was awake. During one of these waking periods, just as the sun dropped below the horizon and the sky was beginning to grow dark, Horrocks was able to sit up in bed, leaning back on his elbows, and he was obviously aware of where he was and of what had happened. It was for only a few minutes, and he fell back exhausted, but Gill took it as another positive sign, before Horrocks had another very restless night.

Early the next morning, when Horrocks seemed to be sleeping

peacefully, Gill went out into the bush looking for a large puddle of rainwa-ter that Bernard Kilroy had found at lunchtime on the day of the accident. Their supply of fresh water was dwindling and, while he knew that Kilroy would bring some back when he returned, he also knew that it was far bet-ter to have too much than not enough in a land such as this. He was unable to locate Kilroy's puddle but, rather than waste the trip, he walked out onto the bed of the lake named in his honour to collect saltwater instead. It was undrinkable, but it would be useful in bathing Horrocks' wounds.

When he returned to the tent, he found Horrocks awake and, to Gill, he seemed to be a little bit better today than he had been yesterday; he seemed, at least, to be a lot more composed. In contrast to this, Gill him-self felt terrible, exhausted by a lack of sleep complicated by the anxiety he still felt about Horrocks.

Horrocks was able to speak now, although it obviously caused him pain to do so. His speech was slow and tortuous, but at least he and Gill could hold a conversation. In answer to Horrocks' question, Gill said that the earliest he expected Kilroy and any others to return was the morn-ing of the next day, which would be Friday, 4 September. When talking about this, Horrocks expressed real concerns about the possibility of Kilroy even reaching Depot Creek, saying that he would have to travel at least 70 miles through the scrub with no real likelihood of finding any fresh water along the route. Gill could see the subject was upsetting to Horrocks, so he spoke of other things until, predictably, John Horrocks once again drifted off to sleep.

After another restless night, Horrocks fell into a deep sleep shortly before dawn. When he awoke several hours later, Gill helped him to drink some lukewarm tea and then bathed his face. When Horrocks slipped back into sleep, Gill left him and again went out into the scrub, this time heading directly north from the camp. Once more, he trekked for one mile, then two, but found no traces of water anywhere. When he returned to the campsite, he could hear Horrocks calling out his name from the tent.

Horrocks urgently wanted to get out from that tent. Whether this was to attend to various calls of nature or simply to relieve the sense of confinement he must have been feeling is unclear, but Gill managed to get him dressed and the two men went for a short walk around the campsite, a short walk interrupted by many rest breaks for the wounded man. Horrocks remained out of bed for half an hour, and when he was again reclining, Gill shaved him and again changed his dressings, replacing the poultice on his facial wound for the third time.

Afterwards, Horrocks sat up in bed and the two men talked. They were still talking when they had heard the unmistakeable sound of hoof beats and at around 1.30 p.m., Bernard Kilroy and John Theakston arrived at the campsite. The relief was palpable for both Gill and Horrocks. The men had brought arrowroot to help Horrocks' recovery, and after preparing a draught for him, they held a brief conference. Horrocks would never fully recover in a tent in the desert, and it was important that he be given the best medical assistance available, and that he be given it as soon as possible. There was no arguing with the logic of this. The campsite was quickly packed up, the camel loaded and the trip back to Depot Creek begun, John Horrocks riding when he could, resting when he couldn't. After five miles, they stopped for the night.

The rescue party continued their journey at 7 a.m. the next morning. They travelled quickly in three distinct stages, resting for half an hour between each stage. They would pause if Horrocks asked to rest, but such pauses were rare as he seemed to realise that speed was critical at this time. At each halt, they gave Horrocks a draught of arrowroot. After covering around 25 miles, they made their camp at a spot where they had found water on the outward trip. There was not as much water there now, but fortunately there was just enough for the men and the animals.

It was just on dusk when they halted. The condition of the horses as much as the condition of the men dictated when they came to a stop. For the horses, this was the first water since the last time they had stopped there more than 30 hours previously. They had also eaten very little since leaving Depot Creek, so they were badly in need of food and rest, as were the men. Horrocks was completely exhausted by the time they stopped, but only slept for short periods during the night. The other three men were not much better, but Gill made a gallon of tea when they arrived at the campsite, and they all slept well.

The next morning was Sunday 6 September and the men were again up at dawn, anxious to see if they could make it back to Depot Creek that day. They were trekking as soon as their camp was dismantled and again tried to make the best time they could. Horrocks continued to ride one of the horses and Theakston the other, but this day Kilroy and Gill took it in turns to ride the camel. When one was riding Harry, the other would be leading him. In this way, they were able to maintain a steady average of four miles an hour, even though the day's travel was not just through the scrub, but up and down sand ridges and sand hills as well.

The little party stopped for half an hour at 11 a.m. and again at three in the afternoon, and arrived at Depot Creek at 6 p.m., all very sore and tired. Horrocks had held up well that day, but they had all pushed hard and were more than happy to reach their destination. *"This,"* wrote Gill, *"made the supper and bed a very desirable termination to our trying tramp."*

*   *   *

For this week at least, Monday rather than Sunday was their day of rest and all those at Depot Creek took the opportunity to recuperate from what had gone before while preparing for what lay ahead. Theakston said that he believed, if the message had been successfully passed on by

William Garlick, Dr. Brown might arrive that day or the next. Horrocks seemed to have recovered from the trip, if not the wounds, but expressed some concern over what the long-term implications of his missing middle finger might be. Samuel Gill had a shorter-term concern; that morning, he bathed himself, noting in his journal that it was the first time he had bathed in seven days.

It was back to business on Tuesday morning. The previous evening, just on dusk, one of their horses had disappeared and, after breakfast, Theakston, Gill and Jimmy Moorhouse all went out searching for it; all returned without any sighting of the missing animal. While they were away, Bernard Kilroy spent the morning shoeing the other horses. A lunchtime meeting determined there was nothing to recommend remaining at Depot Creek. Had Dr. Brown been coming, he should have been there by now. The new plan was to allow the horses to improve their condition and to depart for Penwortham in two days' time. Further decisions could be made there.

John Horrocks also dictated and signed a letter that day at Depot Creek. Addressed to Edward Platt, the honorary secretary of the Northern Expedition, and headed "Depot Creek, 8 September," it opened, "*It is with the greatest regret I have to inform the committee and my fellow colonists who subscribed towards the expenses of its untimely and unfortunate termination...*"

The body of the letter was devoted to an appreciation of what the expedition had found, and what Horrocks surmised about it all. He stated his belief that it was improbable that pastoral enterprises could ever be established to the west of Lake Torrens. All the rain that fell there drained into lakes which dried up completely a few days after it had fallen.

Horrocks went on. If the accident had not occurred, it had been his plan to push up through some low country he had spotted off to the north-east. Following that, he would have circled Lake Torrens, a journey he estimated would have covered between 300 and 400 miles. But it was not to be, and he noted that when he had arrived back at Depot Creek, all — including the camel and horses — had been in a bad shape.

Horrocks ended the letter with his usual mixture of realism and hope:

"…it is with extreme sorrow that I am obliged to terminate the expedition as the two men that were with me, the camel and myself were in excellent working condition. Had it been earlier in the season and my wounds healed up, I should have started again."

Early the next morning, the missing horse trotted back into camp and resumed its place grazing with the others as though nothing had happened. Samuel Gill went to the top of one of the nearby hills to sketch the countryside around the camp. John Horrocks spent much of the day resting in his tent, emerging at semi-regular intervals to stretch his legs or to converse with one or more of the others. They all agreed that he seemed to be growing a little stronger with each passing day.

*   *   *

Thursday 10 September may well have been the most miserable day of the entire expedition, at least as far as the weather was concerned. It was a grey and cool day; the clouds seemed to be sitting on the Flinders Ranges, and they trekked through intermittent showers for most of the day as they again retraced their earlier steps. Packing up their base camp in the morning took more time than it should have and one consequence of this was that they did not leave Depot Creek until it was at least 9.30. They also stopped early, on the edge of quite a large creek around five miles north of Mount Brown. Theakston estimated that they had travelled around 19 miles that day.

As a result of discussions held that evening, changes were afoot the next morning. Horrocks and Kilroy would depart as soon as they could and ride direct to Malcolm Campbell's station. With luck, they would find Dr. Brown waiting for them there. If not, they would continue towards Penwortham, travelling at whatever pace Horrocks found comfortable and seeking assistance in the districts they travelled through, districts that now contained a number of large pastoral properties. It seems there must have been some concerns about whether Horrocks' wounds were actually improving. The others would travel at their own pace, largely determined by the drays and the livestock.

The rest of the party, now led by John Theakston, packed up and were moving shortly after 8 a.m. With the real urgency now gone from their travelling, they were able to move at a pace dictated mainly by the drays. They stopped early at a watercourse they had previously named Stoney Creek, where they found an abundance of fresh water and plenty of pasturage for the livestock. There was also an abundance of game in the form of kangaroos and emus. Willing to give the greyhounds one more chance, Gill took them out hunting. Not unsurprisingly, the experiment was again an abject failure.

The next day continued at the same easy pace. After filling their water barrels in the creek, the travellers continued on their journey. During the day they passed through the most pleasant country where there were again numbers of kangaroos and emu; almost against his better judgement, Gill took the dogs out among them. He was no longer surprised by the result. They later took a break alongside a free-flowing creek, which Gill sketched, and then proceeded to cross some very rough and broken ground.

That ground took longer to cross than they expected, and they decided to camp on the southern boundary of the patch as soon as they had made a successful crossing. Setting up the camp took only a short time — they were very experienced at it now — but when they had completed that task, one of them pointed out that there was no sign of the goats. Jimmy

Moorhouse was usually responsible for them but, since they departed Depot Creek, his main responsibility had become the camel while Theakston and Gill looked after the drays. The goats usually trotted along with the main party, and all three were certain the goats had been with them when they entered the rough ground. The men searched until dark but found no trace of the missing animals.

The following day was a Sunday, the 13th of September, and the three men made no plans to move on again that day. Instead they were up early searching for the missing goats. No-one could find any trace of them, and even Jimmy Moorhouse admitted that it looked like they had simply vanished into thin air. If there was any consolation, it was that Gill shot a kangaroo while searching for the goats. When the three returned to the camp at lunchtime, he took his pony out to bring back the carcase. Jimmy Moorhouse also had some good fortune that afternoon when he, too, shot a kangaroo that had wandered close to their campsite.

There was further trouble with livestock the next morning when the men found that the horses had wandered off during the night. Fortunately, Theakston and Jimmy Moorhouse soon found and recovered them. Although they broke camp a little later at 9 a.m., they still managed to cover 30 miles that day. What made that figure even more impressive was that much of it was through thick scrub, which proved especially heavy going for the oxen pulling the drays. There was no water for the animals either, but an hour before dusk they encountered a pasture of good grass and stopped there for the night.

The men knew they were drawing close to the outer limits of settlement, so they pushed hard again the next day. They were on the move by 7.30 a.m., but the pace proved a bit much for Samuel Gill who went lame in his left foot from "too much walking", as he described the condition. He also pointed out that the only reason he had been walking at all was because his pony had a sore back and he didn't want to aggravate it any further. They made good time again this day and at 5.30 p.m. arrived at the boundary of a run owned by a man named Ferguson. They camped by the stream which marked that boundary.

They were on the road again by 7.30 the following morning and had not travelled far before they were intercepted by the station owner, Mr. Ferguson, himself. He had ridden some ten miles from his homestead to see if he could be of any assistance and to bring them news of John Horrocks. It seemed that no doctor was either willing or able to travel this far into the wilderness to treat him, and he and Kilroy were slowly making their way back to Penwortham. It also sounded as though Horrocks' condition was unchanged from the last time they had seen him. The men thanked Ferguson, who left them to return to his homestead, and they continued south, stopping that night at Hope's station. It was a hard night to be camping out, with unabated heavy rain throughout.

That heavy rain continued into and through the next day, convincing the little group that their best course of action was to stay where they were. If nothing else, the break allowed Gill the opportunity to treat his lame foot with marshmallow, followed by rest. It was, he wrote, "much eased" by nightfall. They moved on again the next morning, Friday 18 September, when, like Gill's foot, the weather was much improved. They passed through both the Watts and Hawker stations that day, and camped the night at Magpie Flat, also the site of one of their earlier stopovers.

Knowing they were now almost at their objective, there was not a lot of urgency in their movements on the Saturday morning. They left Magpie Flat shortly after 8 a.m. and arrived at Penwortham at midday. Once there, they set up camp behind the mill and made enquiries after Horrocks and his well-being. A very sick John Horrocks had arrived in Penwortham just a couple of days earlier. As Hope Farm had been let during his absence, he was taken to the home of a friend, Edgar Bold Robinson, and he had been given his own room there. John Green had assumed responsibility for Horrocks' personal care; he washed and changed him and made Horrocks as comfortable as he could.

Since Horrocks arrived and took his place in bed in the main room of Robinson's house, a regular procession of visitors had called in to pay their respects to the village's founder. Horrocks spoke to them all, giving them little details about what he had seen on his Northern Expedition. Most who visited came away believing he was over the worst and would undoubtedly live. That was why John Theakston was so surprised when John Green told him that Horrocks was too sick to see anyone, even someone as close to him as Theakston.

In the early evening, Arthur Horrocks and Dr. John Knott arrived up from Adelaide and went straight to see John Horrocks. Afterwards, Arthur went to stay with the rest of the exploring party in their camp at the mill. Dr. Knott was offered a room at the Robinson house. This gave him a chance to undertake a thorough medical examination of Horrocks. After that examination, and with a heavy heart, Knott began drafting in his head the letter he would begin to write the next day to Horrocks' widowed mother in London. In it, he would say that he did not believe her eldest son, John, would survive the injuries he had suffered.

*   *   *

John Horrocks' condition was unchanged the following day, and he was still not up to seeing visitors. Knott saw him again, and the two men spoke for a while, Horrocks speaking of the expedition and the accident and telling the doctor that Gill had saved his life: "*His attention could not have been surpassed. He was a brave and steady companion.*" While that was undoubtedly true, Knott was increasingly concerned by Horrocks current state of health, especially the mangled stump of his middle finger which appeared to have turned gangrenous.

Knott believed he would need to operate on the infected area, removing the stump of the finger and perhaps the rest of the hand, but also believed he would need another doctor to assist him in that surgery. At his request, Arthur Horrocks and John Green went to fetch a Dr. Campbell, who must have lived somewhere in those northern districts. The men returned early in the afternoon to say that Campbell had not been at home but that they had sent one of his men off to request his presence at Robinson's house early the next morning.

With not a lot else to do, the men spent the afternoon in and around the camp at the rear of the mill. Edgar Robinson and Knott viewed Gill's sketches and paintings, complimenting the artist on their quality. It was later reported that Horrocks' health suffered a relapse during the evening.

*   *   *

There was no change to Horrocks' increasingly precarious position on Monday morning. Bernard Kilroy had been attending him overnight and returned to the explorers' campsite shortly after dawn. He was replaced by Arthur Horrocks, who would remain with his brother during the daylight hours. John Green would also be there should further assistance be required. When there was no sign of Dr. Campbell during the morning, John Theakston volunteered to go and collect him. Brooking no arguments, Theakston returned with Campbell late in the afternoon. While he was on this errand, the others packed away most of the camp and took up residence in the mill. When he arrived, Knott took Campbell to see Horrocks immediately and afterwards walked across to the mill to inform the others that Dr. Campbell agreed with his prognosis; John Horrocks was now dangerously ill.

Horrocks' health deteriorated even further during the night and both Arthur and Horrocks' friends now feared for his life. John Theakston and Jimmy Moorhouse had planned to ride down to Adelaide that day with the news from the expedition, but Horrocks' delicately-balanced health seemed more important than that and they elected to stay at Penwortham.

During the morning, Theakston was admitted into Horrocks' room for the first time since they had all returned from the north. He would have been shocked at the sight of his friend and fellow explorer, but Horrocks himself seemed to cope with the situation far better than anyone else in the room. There were several there, of course; Dr. Knott was there seeing to his friend and patient and, in the absence of the clergyman that Horrocks had been so determined to bring to Penwortham, John Jacobs led the prayers and attended as well as he could to his friend's spiritual needs.

If John Horrocks' body was gradually shutting down, his mind remained clear and his thoughts were lucid. Spotting Theakston as he entered, he called his second in command over and, as silent tears fell down most of the faces in the room, he outlined just how his burial was to be conducted. He identified precisely where he was to be buried in the plot of land he had gifted to the people of Penwortham, and asked that his grave be bricked in. There were other details as well and, in conclusion, he dictated what he wanted on his gravestone and asked Theakston, as a personal favour, to carve the words himself. With his earthly business concluded, Horrocks lapsed into a laboured sleep.

Seeing that there was no more that he could do, Dr. Knott rode off to Adelaide during the afternoon, firm in the belief that John Horrocks would not last through the night. As he was riding south, many of Adelaide's citizens were reading that day's edition of the *South Australian*. One item in it noted that news had been received from Robinson's station on 18 September. The explorer John Horrocks and his party had recently arrived there. It had been further reported that Horrocks had been accidentally wounded; the wounds, however, were not considered serious, although it was thought that his injured right hand might need to be amputated.

*   *   *

On the morning of Wednesday 23 September 1846, John Horrocks' physical condition had really changed only by slight degrees from the night before. The troubled sleep had become a coma that deepened as the day wore on. That in turn became a deep coma during the morning, and his breathing slowed and became shallower as the afternoon progressed. Shortly after dusk, his body was wracked with pain and he began to experience convulsions. At the end of one of these, his body went still. His heart just stopped as John Horrocks began a new journey to the other side of another mountain.

The Other Side of the Mountain

John Ainsworth Horrocks, aged 28, was buried the day following his death. He was the first to be interred in the graveyard that would become part of the St Mark's Church of England establishment in Penwortham. His burial was thus too early for parish records, but we know its details from the recollections of those who attended. The funeral took place at 5.30 p.m. and commenced when his coffin was carried from the carriage in which it had been brought from the Robinson house to the grave which had been prepared to receive it. In accordance with the tradition for burying explorers, the grave was aligned on a north-south axis. It was also in the exact spot that Horrocks had requested.

The pallbearers who carried the coffin were all villagers from Penwortham, many of whom had followed Horrocks to the other side of the world from the original Penwortham Hall in Lancashire. The coffin was followed by the 40 or more mourners who attended the burial, led by Arthur Horrocks and including those who had accompanied him on that last Northern Expedition as well as the friends he had made in the few short years he had lived a life at the edge of civilization. Again, in the absence of a clergyman, the funeral service of the Church of England was led by Horrocks' friend, John Jacobs.

The coffin was lowered into the grave, soil was thrown on it, and then the mourners stood back as Jimmy Moorhouse led Harry the camel to a position alongside Horrocks' grave. It was said that, as he lay dying, John Horrocks asked that Harry be put down after his own death, not as an act of revenge against the animal that most held responsible for his death, but because he feared the animal would be mistreated for the rest of its life because of what had happened. Whatever the reality and whatever the reason, a future first mayor of Clare and friend of the Horrocks family, E.B. "Paddy" Gleeson had volunteered to put Harry down.

As Jimmy Moorhouse held Harry's lead, Gleeson stepped forward, raised his gun, and fired into the camel's body. His hands were visibly shaking as he did so and the musket ball he fired missed all the animal's vital organs. Harry, suddenly hurt and frightened, reared up in the air, and then struck out at the nearest person, Jimmy Moorhouse. As Harry bit into Moorhouse's scalp, another Penwortham resident named Darmody, also stepped forward. Perhaps anticipating such a possibility, he was armed as well and, as the mourners jumped back in fright and Jimmy Moorhouse screamed in pain, Darmody fired a single bullet into Harry's heart, killing him instantly.

The carnage at the gravesite ended the funeral. Mrs. Gleeson treated Jimmy Moorhouse's wounds, which were quite severe. She washed them out, then bandaged them, while her husband and several volunteers used horses to drag Harry's body to a position below an extremely large gum tree where he, too, would later be buried. At the end, when John Horrocks and his little expedition were in the wastes beyond the Flinders Ranges, Horrocks was the only one who believed that Harry and other camels like him probably held the secret to opening up the interior of Australia. Perhaps he thought, too, that those who had shown a way forward should spend eternity together as well.

Widely admired in life, especially in the northern reaches of the colony, John Horrocks was also widely commemorated and eulogised in death.

More than 40 years after his passing, Clare's *Northern Argus* would still fondly recall one of the district's pioneers as being, *"Of noble form, frank, of courteous bearing and kindly disposition, he was an admirable specimen of an English country gentleman, and his untimely death was deeply lamented by a large circle of friends, but by the colonists generally."*

The loss was felt even as far afield as his country of birth. When news of Horrocks' death reached England, Lady Frances Hotham, wife of a Napoleonic wars' naval hero, daughter of an earl and childhood friend of the Horrocks family, wrote to John's best friend and favourite sister, Celia.

"John Horrocks will ever live in my memory as one of the noblest specimens, both in mind and body, of the human species."

Shortly after the funeral, John Green returned to England. His reasons for doing so were twofold. He wanted to visit his elderly parents to tell them that his life was now in South Australia and to therefore say goodbye to them both. He also wanted to spend time with the Horrocks family, to tell them about John's last days and to pass on any final messages John had entrusted to him. As luck would have it, Clara Horrocks and her children were off on one of their grand tours of Europe. He followed them from place to place, eventually catching up with them in Vienna, where he delivered the news and, in doing so, performed the last act of a lifetime of service to the Horrocks family.

John Green returned to South Australia, to the northern districts he had come to love and to the farm he had built for himself and his family at Skillogolee Creek, not all that far from Penwortham. There he died on 212 June 1862; he was aged just 47 years. His devotion to the Horrocks family may have been forgotten, but his name has not. Green's Bridge, a couple of kilometres to the south of Clare, is named after him.

*   *   *

On 30 November 1851, St Mark's Anglican Church in Penwortham was consecrated by Bishop Augustus Short, South Australia's first Anglican bishop. The occasion was celebrated by the ringing of the church's bell, the self-same bell that John Horrocks had brought to Australia 12 years earlier. In the intervening years it had lain unused and in storage until presented to the church by Mr. and Mrs. Arthur Horrocks on behalf of John. The church was, and remains, the oldest Anglican building in South Australia to the north of Gawler.

A marble tablet commemorating John Horrocks' short life was placed on the church's wall at the family's direction and at the family's expense. At the top of the tablet was set a golden eagle, the symbol of ascension, holding something red in its beak. Underneath this was the family motto, "Industria et spe," which is Latin for "By faith and works". Below that were John's name and birthplace and an inscription.

"Landed in South Australia the day he came of age, A.D. 1839; died September 23, 1846, from a wound accidentally received from his own gun during his exploring expeditions north of Spencer's Gulf.

Blessed are they that die in the Lord."

Later, and again at the family's direction, the words *"from his own gun"* were scored from the tablet as it was feared by them that people unfamiliar with John Horrocks' fate might assume that he had taken his own life.

*   *   *

Sometime after his brother's death, Arthur Horrocks married Ann Jacobs, the sister of one of John's best friends at Penwortham. Arthur and Ann moved into the main house at Hope Farm, and started a family while living there. Arthur was not cut out to be a farmer, though. His damaged leg limited what he could do physically and, temperamentally, he was a man of the city and of commerce. While living at Penwortham, he served as a councillor alongside the town mayor, Paddy Gleeson. After a decade at Hope Farm and Penwortham, Arthur and his family moved south to Adelaide.

Arthur Horrocks died at his home in North Adelaide on 7 July 1872. Newspaper records suggest that he and Ann had at least three sons and that one of them was the father of another John Ainsworth Horrocks. That John Horrocks, a second lieutenant in the Australian Army, was killed in action on the Western front on 11 August 1918.

Unoccupied after the departure of Arthur Horrocks and his family, the farmhouse at Hope Farm subsequently fell into disrepair and then ruin. What remained of it was cleared when the Riverton-Spalding railway was constructed over the spot where it had once stood.

*   *   *

Bernard Kilroy, Jimmy Moorhouse and William Garlick all disappeared from the pages of history after the fatal end of John Horrocks' Northern Expedition. Horrocks' other companions on that venture left some traces behind.

Dr. John Knott, who backed the expedition with his own money and who was both a friend and a physician to John Horrocks, died in an accident four years later. One winter's night in 1850, Knott called in to the Butcher's Arms Hotel in Thebarton. He arrived around 8 p.m., obviously affected by alcohol, tied his horse to the hitching post outside and strode into the hotel. At the bar, he asked the landlady for a brandy and water. She replied that she thought that he'd probably already had enough, and that if he had any more he wouldn't be fit to ride home.

Sensing that the situation was about to turn nasty, one of the hotel staff, a stable hand, stepped behind the bar and poured two glasses of hot brandy and water. The stable hand drank his straight down, but the landlady reached across to the other glass and emptied it into a tub of dirty water. At this, Knott glared at the woman then turned and left the hotel. Outside, he unhitched and mounted his horse and rode off. He quickly spurred the horse into a gallop but had travelled only a short distance when a stirrup broke and he was thrown off. Knott's skull was badly fractured in the fall. He did not regain consciousness and died the next morning.

Sometime after that event, John Theakston left Adelaide for Victoria, probably to try his luck on the goldfields there. His descendants believe he may also have been in receipt of some financial support from the Horrocks family in England. He married, had children, including at least one son who took up residence in Port Lincoln. Theakston, apparently now living alone, applied for admission to an Old Colonists Home in Victoria in 1870, and in December 1877, was admitted to the Ararat Asylum, where he died the following March.

Samuel Thomas Gill remained in Adelaide for several more years, opening another, larger studio in Leigh Street. He, too, moved to Victoria at the time of the gold rushes there and there also painted some of his most famous works. Increasingly dependent on alcohol to chase the shadows away, he slowly slipped into unemployment and destitution. S.T. Gill dropped dead on the steps of the Melbourne GPO in 1880 and was buried in a nameless pauper's grave.

*   *   *

A full account of the expedition was later recorded by the Surveyor General's Office in Adelaide. In May 1919, the South Australian Public Library Board received a diary from Celia Temple, nee Horrocks, and John Horrocks' sister. The diary, written in the form of a manuscript, was based around the letters that Horrocks had written to Celia. It also contained a biographical sketch of his life and a map of his final expedition. The material was handed over by Charles Horrocks, the explorer's nephew.

A 100th anniversary of Penwortham service was held at St Mark's Church in October 1939. After the service, a 'pilgrimage' was made to John Horrocks' grave where the chairman of the Clare District Council laid a commemorative wreath.

On the eve of the centenary of John Horrocks' death, three memorial cairns were unveiled in the northern districts. The first, built of local stone, was alongside the main road at Penwortham, the spot from where the Northern Expedition departed in July 1846. The second, constructed from pink stone, is at the southern end of Horrocks Pass. The third, made of Indian granite, was built at the junction of the Main North Road and Port Pirie Road, along the route that Horrocks followed.

Lake Gill does not appear on any modern map, nor is there any marker nearby to indicate the high point of John Horrocks' Northern Expedition and, perhaps, his life. The lake was rediscovered by another explorer in 1858 and he gave it the name it still carries, Lake Dutton, named after Mr. F.S. Dutton, at one time Agent General for South Australia in London. The traveller can, though, drive past Mount Horrocks, outside Penwortham, to the Horrocks Highway, looking out across the Gulnare Plains and Magpie Flat, crossing the Stoney Creek and traversing the Flinders Ranges via Horrocks Pass, so John Horrocks, the explorer has not been entirely forgotten. And yet....

A week after his death, the South Australian *Register* said that John Horrocks' *"...unavailing regret was that the fatal bird should have intercepted his progress just at the time he and his companions were reaching the district he felt so anxious to explore."*

Had he lived, had the accident at Lake Gill given him a fright instead of a mortal wound, he would have found that there was not all that much beyond Lake Torrens. But he would have gone again, and again after that.

By definition, explorers are persons who travel beyond where previous people have travelled. Equally, someone must have at some earlier time gone to where the explorer started from, someone provided the base on which that explorer built. In Australian history, the names of the great explorers roll off the historian's tongue: Lawson, Wentworth and Blaxland, Charles Sturt, Ludwig Leichhardt, the Gregorys and Edward John Eyre. Each of them went where other Europeans had not been before; each started from a point that an earlier explorer had found.

Had John Horrocks or, for that matter, John Darke, lived through their final explorations their names may also have been added to that list. An argument can be made that Horrocks' name should already be there. A pass through a mountain range, a lake and a few plains and hills do not qualify him on most accounts. What does is Harry, the camel. On his Northern Expedition, Horrocks showed that a camel could cover 25 miles or more a day, in desert and semi-desert country carrying loads of up to 350 pounds weight. It was something that Burke and Wills learned of and used on their own ill-fated journey north 14 years later. It was also something that those who exploited the explorers' discoveries learned from John Horrocks as well, and it is arguable that much of Australia's inland wealth and development can be traced back to one man and one camel.

Had they lived, this; had they lived, that. The argument is both circular and pointless. Neither John Horrocks nor Harry the camel survived a fairly minor exploration into the desert fringes of the South Australian colony. Their short lives and unusual deaths became a footnote to history, and that footnote does justice to neither the man nor the beast. They were the first at what they did, pioneers whose achievements have been subsumed by others. That does not diminish what they achieved and what they meant. It just allows us to appreciate it all the more.

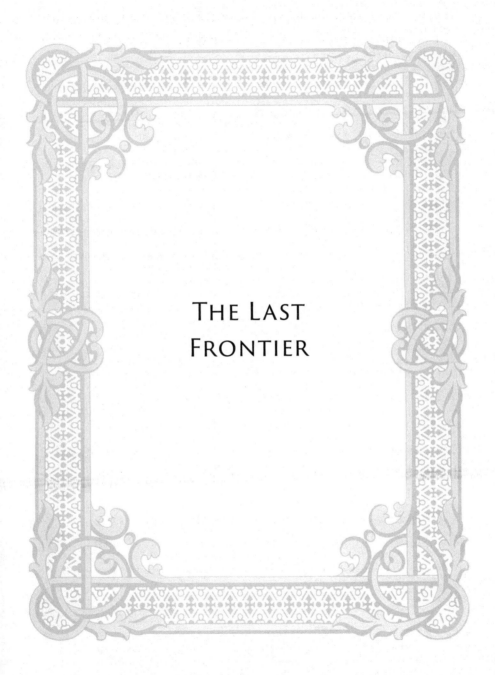

THE LAST
FRONTIER

BIRTHRIGHTS

Horatio Spencer Howe Wills was born at home in Sydney on 3 October 1811, almost five months to the day after the death of his father, Edward Spencer Wills. The home in which he was born was a substantial building at 96 George Street, then the heart of the bustling little town's commercial district. That house needed to be substantial; not only was it home to a growing family of Wills' children, it was the centre of Edward and Sarah Wills' growing business empire, a business with interests across the colony of New South Wales, south to Van Diemen's Land and the islands of Bass Strait, and east into the vast expanses of the Pacific Ocean.

That business had been built from scratch by a man who would die before his 33rd birthday, whose working life in his native London had been as a lowly-paid printer and who had, around the time of his 19th birthday, stood in a dock, charged with highway robbery, and listened to a bewigged judge tell him that his guilt for the crime meant that he would be taken from the dock and, at a subsequent date, be hanged by the neck until dead.

* * *

Edward Wills sped through life. Born in London in 1778, he was apprenticed to a printer named Millar Ritchie as soon as he was old enough to start work. At 16 years of age, he met Sarah Harding, who was two years older than him. The young couple fell in love and married in London in 1795; Sarah was 19 years old and her husband just 17. Nine months and two weeks after the marriage, the couple's first child arrived, a little girl they named Sarah. Whether the additional financial demands of a family made a difference is something that cannot be ascertained, but something in Edward's life made him turn to crime. In early 1797, Edward Wills, James Dashper and another man robbed three citizens at gunpoint at Longacre in London, stealing eleven shillings, nine pence and a watch.

All three were arrested soon afterward, while the money and watch were found at Edward's home. The men were charged with highway robbery in March 1797, found guilty and sentenced to death by hanging. The families of the three all appealed the sentences handed down. Wills' family argued vigorously for clemency, pointing out what they believed to be several salient points. It was Edward Wills' first offence, they said, and he came from a good family. Moreover, he was recently married and already had a young family. Added to his family's pleas was a testimonial from his employer, Millar Ritchie. On 29 March, the death sentences on all three men were commuted to transportation for life to New South Wales, about as far away from London as it was possible to go.

After a voyage of 218 days from London, the convict transport *Hillsborough* arrived in Sydney on 26 July 1799. Aboard were 300 convicts who had been sentenced to transportation to New South Wales for periods that varied from seven years to life. One of those convicts was the highwayman, Edward Spencer Wills. Also aboard the *Hillsborough* were Sarah Wills and the couple's three-year-old daughter. There were formalities to be attended to, but these were over in a few days. As a free settler, Sarah Wills was eligible to have working convicts assigned to her to help her establish herself in the colony. She asked for only one, her husband, and as the new century loomed over the horizon, Edward and Sarah looked to begin a new life for themselves and their family.

*   *   *

Edward and Sarah began their business life together as traders, buying whatever they thought they could sell at a profit, no matter how small that profit might have been. They were obviously good at what they did as their business began to grow and to make good money. When Edward was granted a conditional pardon, or Ticket of Leave, in June 1803, things began to develop on several fronts as he was now able to earn and conduct business in his own right rather than as his wife's assigned servant. There were many others like Edward in Sydney at that time, former convicts who had determined that the colony offered them the opportunity to make a clean break from their past in a new society. While that society was not exactly classless, it was a society where it was possible for a man, or a woman, to ascend through its striations by dint of hard work rather than because of the circumstances of their birth.

Opportunities existed in abundance in Sydney. Not yet 25 years old, New South Wales would struggle to claim that it was self-sufficient in anything. Most of what was used in everyday life had to be imported, and those who knew the ins and outs of successful trading could achieve real wealth in a relatively short time. Edward and Sarah were two such traders. When they could afford to, they bought a substantial brick home at 96 George Street as a family home. It was large enough to also house their business and agreeably close to the docks and warehouses that now crowded around the shores of Sydney Cove.

Their business enterprises moved to a new level in 1805 when, in September, Edward went into a commercial partnership with Thomas

Reibey, a free settler and former trader with the East India Company who, with his ex-convict wife Mary, was also looking to grow his business. Wills and Reibey wanted to exploit the seal trade in and around the Bass Strait islands as both seal oil and seal fur were attracting high prices in Sydney as well as in the export markets. They initially purchased a single boat, but the immediate success of the venture saw them purchase a second. The next year, they bought a third vessel, a schooner named the *Mercury*, specifically for trade with the Pacific Islands.

The success of the sealing and Pacific Island trading ventures allowed Edward and Sarah to diversify their business interests. They bought a working farm at Prospect, then beyond the limits of settlement, and built a farmhouse there. In time, it would provide fresh produce for the Sydney market. They also built their own warehouse on the docks of Sydney Cove as the volume their business was generating had far outgrown their capacity to run it from their home in George Street. Using the new warehouse did free up a lot of space in that home, space that was converted for use firstly as a tavern and later as a fashionable restaurant.

As the Wills' business prospered, the family grew apace. Thomas — called Tom by his family — was born in 1800, and was followed by Eliza in 1802, Edward in 1805 and Elizabeth in 1808. In 1810, Edward Spencer Wills was granted a full pardon and became one of what were referred to as "emancipists", a class of former convicts starting to emerge as a distinct, Australian-oriented social class. Around the same time, Edward became aware that his health was failing and that he may not have long to live. Late in 1810, he drew up a last will and testament and made other financial arrangements for his estate.

In January 1811, there was a new urgency in the Wills household. With Edward's health visibly declining, they sold the farm and farmhouse at Prospect to help consolidate their holdings. Tragedy also struck that month with the death of little Elizabeth Wills at just three years of age.

As if in recompense, Sarah also fell pregnant in January. That child was a son who Edward would not live to see. His health continued to decline, and Edward Spencer Wills died at home on 14 May. He was just 32 years old when he passed away, but his will included assets valued at in excess of 15,000 pounds, an enormous amount at that time. For a man sentenced to hang for the theft of less than a pound, Edward Wills had done very well indeed.

*   *   *

Horatio Spencer Howe Wills was born to a father he would never know and was christened with a name he would rarely use. When he was old enough, he would refer to himself as Horace rather than Horatio. There was no reason ever attributed to this. Similarly, the name Howe was given to the baby in recognition of George Howe, his father's friend and business partner in several ventures. The reason that he would drop Howe from his name would be readily apparent over time.

*   *   *

In 1812, the widow Sarah Wills married George Howe, who was then the owner, publisher and printer of the *Sydney Gazette*, the colony's first newspaper. Another ex-convict and a printer by trade, Howe was appointed as the Government Printer by Governor King in 1803. It seems Howe's printing abilities exceeded his moral compass by some distance, as Howe's life reveals he was always on the lookout for the main chance. Howe and his first wife had a son they named Robert, born in England in 1795, shortly before Howe was sentenced to life transportation to New South Wales after being found guilty of robbery. Howe's wife and son sailed with him for Sydney, but Mrs. Howe did not survive the voyage.

In Sydney, Howe entered into a de facto relationship with a woman named Elizabeth, a relationship which produced five children — one of whom died in infancy — between 1803 and 1810. The following year, after the death of his friend and associate Edward Wills, Howe simply walked out on Elizabeth in order to court the newly bereaved Sarah Wills. Howe and Sarah married in 1812, and soon after Howe and all his surviving children, moved in with Sarah and her children at 96 George Street. In November 1816, the couple had their only child together, a daughter they named Jane.

From the distance of over two centuries, it is impossible to assess the strength of the marriage, but it was certainly one with secrets. George Howe also suffered from failing health and in March 1821, he drew up a will in which he left everything he owned to Sarah. Two months later he drew up a second, secret will in which he left his printing business to his son Robert, with everything else to be divided between his four illegitimate children, Horace Wills and Sarah Howe. Within a few days, George Howe was dead. Sarah challenged the secret will, and the case was still before the courts when Sarah herself died suddenly in 1823. The final outcome of the disputed will was a court decision that all the family assets should be held in trust for Sarah's children.

*   *   *

The early deaths of both Edward and Sarah Wills had an immediate and drastic impact on their children. While those children would carry emotional scars from the twin traumas for the remainder of their lives, the business success that their parents had crafted meant that those lives would not have to be lived in poverty. The family's wealth and increasing connections would also allow them opportunities not available to the less fortunate in colonial New South Wales.

Two months after Edward Wills' death, his oldest daughter, Sarah, married the prominent Sydney doctor, William Redfern. Redfern, who was then around 36 years of age, was a naval surgeon implicated in a mutiny in 1797 and was sentenced to death for his role. That sentence was commuted to transportation to New South Wales for life, and he arrived in Sydney in 1801. After serving as a doctor on Norfolk Island, Redfern returned to Sydney as an assistant surgeon at the Sydney Hospital. He also began a private practice, with the Wills family among his earliest patients.

There seems to have been genuine affection between all the Wills family and Redfern. Sarah Wills was just 14 years old at the time of the marriage, and would remain a lifelong companion for Redfern, whose professional star would continue to rise in the years to come under the patronage of a new governor, Lachlan Macquarie. His personal wealth would also continue to grow, and Redfern was well on the way to becoming one of the colony's wealthiest residents, with extensive landholdings in the suburb which now bears his name and several pastoral properties further out from Sydney. The Redferns would be a constant in Horace's life from the time of his birth.

A second prominent presence would be Horace's oldest brother, Thomas, ten years his senior. Thomas, born in 1800, married firstly into the Reibey family, who by then were almost as wealthy and influential as the Redferns. Unfortunately, Thomas' wife and their baby daughter both died within two years of the marriage. Reeling from the double tragedy, Thomas embarked on an extended overseas trip. Returning to New South Wales, Thomas stopped off at Mauritius, where he met and married his second wife. On the couple's arrival back in Sydney, Thomas decided that they would live on a pastoral property he had purchased at Minto. Two of Horace's sisters also married well into two other prominent pioneering families in colonial New South Wales: the Antills, from an army background; and the Harrisons, from a naval family.

Such family connections were hardly relevant though in Horace's early years, although both Thomas and William Redfern seem to have kept a close eye on his welfare. After some education at home, Horace was sent to a small private school in Sydney. His formal education ended when he was 13, the year after his mother's death, when he was apprenticed as a printer to his stepbrother, Robert Howe, who had taken over the operation of the *Sydney Gazette* upon the death of his father. Robert seems to have inherited some of his father's less flattering characteristics — he was both cantankerous and quarrelsome — and the stepbrothers clashed from almost the minute Horace entered Robert's employ.

By his mid-teens, Horace had reached his adult height of 170 centimetres (5 feet, 7 inches). He wasn't particularly tall and had learned early and quickly to never give in to bullying and to always stand up for himself. He had to, as he and Robert seemed to live most of their shared lives in a state of undeclared warfare. They fought regularly and often, mostly verbal stoushes, some of which would spill over into fistfights. The tensions were exacerbated by the fact that Horace, and several of the other apprentices who worked at the *Gazette*, also boarded with the Howes. Not only were they almost totally dependent on him for food and lodging, there were few opportunities to escape his presence.

When he was 15 years old, Horace ran away from his employment and was absent for several weeks, probably staying with his brother Thomas at Minto. Nothing seems to have changed as a result of this. For some reason, Robert Howe seemed to have disliked all of the Wills family and disliked their patrons even more. He had an especially deep dislike of William Redfern and took every opportunity he could find or manufacture to criticise him in print and in person. Horace's inevitable defence of his brother in law led to further clashes with his stepbrother. Matters finally came to a head when Horace was 17 years old. Howe had written a number of articles critical of his usual targets, but this time had included a thinly veiled attack on his own staff. Horace walked out again, legal action commenced, and the resultant case kept Sydney amused as it unfolded.

In February 1828, Robert Howe took Horace to court alleging that Horace had walked out of his employment before he had completed his indentures. In evidence, Howe said that he believed Horace was also working for another printer. When requested to do so, Howe produced the relevant documents, which were also tendered as evidence. Thomas Wills had engaged a rising young Australian-born lawyer named William Charles Wentworth to defend his young brother, and Wentworth opened that defence by suggesting that ill-treatment at the hands of Howe was a significant factor in the case now before the court. He further claimed that Howe had once thrown a bottle at Horace's head, that he regularly abused him, that Horace was insufficiently fed, and that Howe had even pinioned and horse-whipped Horace.

In cross-examination, Howe admitted to throwing a bottle at Horace and to using what he described as "recriminating expressions" but said that such behaviour had been prompted by Wills' undutiful behaviour. Howe then went on to claim that Horace was, in fact, well-fed, and that they both ate at the same table. He paused, and then went on to say that, in all things, he had always treated Horace Wills as if he were Howe's own son.

A Mr. McLeod was then called as a defence witness by Wentworth. McLeod confirmed the claims already made about what he termed Howe's severe behaviour, in both words and deeds, towards Horace Wills. Despite this type of behaviour occurring regularly, McLeod stated that he had never heard Wills speak of Howe with anything but enthusiasm. A second witness called by Wentworth was another of Howe's apprentices who stated that he, too, was fed far less than he believed was his due. However, in cross-examination, the apprentice admitted that he had never complained to Howe about this and that Howe would therefore not have known of his concerns.

In response to these allegations, Howe stated that the apprentice who had just given evidence did so with animus; he also wanted his indentures cancelled and had recently been sentenced to 14 days' solitary confinement for misconduct. When asked about the meals he supplied to his apprentices, Howe said that their daily allowance was a loaf of two pounds, one pound of meat plus tea and sugar both morning and evening. He added that, if vegetables were not available for dinner, additional bread could be substituted in their place.

Another witness, a Mr. Bourne, stated that Robert Howe's treatment of Horace Wills and his other apprentices was good and was, in fact, far better than the norm for apprentices in England.

After some consultation, the Bench found that Horace Wills' indentures were legal and that he should therefore return to Howe's employment to meet his contractual obligations. Wentworth responded instantly to the finding. He said that, in the first instance, he intended to appeal the finding to a higher body. Until that could be done, he would advise his client to remain living at Dr. Redfern's. As an interim measure, Wentworth continued, he would be seeking a summons to be served on Robert Howe on a charge of mistreating his client over an extended period of time.

The accusations, claims and counter claims continued for months, and Horace did eventually return to work at the *Gazette*. The poisonous relationship he had with his stepbrother ended abruptly in 1829 when Robert Howe drowned in a boating mishap on Sydney Harbour.

*   *   *

The death of Robert Howe pushed Horace into adulthood, a change he seems to have taken in his stride. To begin with, he moved directly from being an apprentice printer to being the proprietor, publisher and printer of one of the colony's major newspapers. That the paper didn't collapse following Howe's death is testament to Horace's industriousness and business acumen. The business also allowed Horace to explore some areas in which he had an interest. One of these was the increasing consciousness of Australia and of Australians as being different to the British stock from which they had sprung.

By the end of the 1820s, almost one quarter of the colony's 35,000 residents had been born locally. Visitors and commentators were beginning to notice that these native-born residents tended to be taller and fairer than the British-born and spoke with what was developing into a distinctive accent. They were also given the name "currency lads and lasses" to distinguish them from the "sterling" citizens born in England; it was something most accepted as an honourable point of distinction. Horace and all but his oldest sibling were Australian born, as were most of the younger members of the circles in which they moved. There was a growing nationalist sentiment as well, something Horace hoped to tap into when he began publication of a new paper, *The Currency Lad*, in August 1828. He was probably a decade too early, for the paper did not capture enough of the public's imagination to survive and ceased publication after just seven months. He may not have grieved over the paper for long, though, as its demise coincided with his growing interest in capturing the affections of a certain young lady.

Her name was Elizabeth and she was a currency lass.

Elizabeth's parents were Michael Wyre and Jane Wallace, Irish convicts transported to New South Wales, who married at Saint John's Church at Parramatta in April 1815. Born in 1817, Elizabeth was the second of the couple's three daughters. When Michael Wyre drowned in a fishing accident in 1823, the three sisters were placed in Parramatta's Female Orphan School. Six-year-old Elizabeth was admitted under the surname McGuire, a name she would keep until her marriage.

Elizabeth and her older sister Catherine were discharged as students from the school in June 1828. Neither left, however, because they were both immediately apprenticed to the school as domestic servants. At the beginning of 1833, Elizabeth entered Mrs. Jane McGillivray's School for Young Ladies; she was just 15 years old. Somewhere and sometime earlier, Elizabeth had met Horace Wills and seems to have made an immediate impression on the young man. Horace could see a future for them and wrote to his brother in law and patron William Redfern in England, where the Redferns were now living.

Redfern replied on 31 October 1832: *"I rejoice to hear that you have sown all your wild oats and that you are determined to become a sensible, steady, clever fellow. To become so only requires resolution."*

Horace had determined to embark on a new direction in his working life as well and was reading texts and talking to those with experience at farming, as he was now convinced that he could achieve success as a pastoralist. This, too, had been mentioned to Redfern, whose advice was to, *"Stick close to your studies and the rest will be sure to follow. If you go on as you promise to do, you will be a credit to yourself, an honour to your relations and a benefit to mankind."*

On 2 December 1832, Elizabeth left Mrs. McGillivray's School for the last time and travelled to Sydney where, at the Scot's Church, she was married to Horace Wills after a courtship that had lasted 18 months. After a brief honeymoon at one of the Antill's properties near Picton, the newlyweds returned to Thomas Wills' farm at Minto where Horace continued to study the basics of agriculture and animal husbandry. Sometime soon, Horace and his new wife would be ready to spread their wings.

LEXINGTON

Horace and Elizabeth Wills' first child, a son they named Thomas Wentworth Wills, was born in a hut on the Molonglo Plains on 19 August 1835. His name paid tribute to two of the men who had been close to Horace for the past decade and more, his older brother Thomas and his legally trained and nationalist friend, William Charles Wentworth. His birth in a hut on the outer margins of the settled country also indicated the path that his parents had chosen for themselves. And, unlike his father, young Tom was to keep his name proudly for the remainder of his life.

After their marriage and a period of learning the theory and practice of farming at the senior Wills' farm at Minto, Horace and Elizabeth moved further to the south-west, to the area then known as the Limestone and Molonglo Plains district, near where the tiny settlement of Queanbeyan had recently sprung into existence. It was a semi-settled rather than a closely settled district at that time; in 1835, a visiting magistrate, a Mr. T. A. Murray, estimated the total European population of the Limestone Plains and the Monaro region further to the south to be no more than 800. Among that number were several related to Horace by marriage, members of the pioneering Antill family.

The Antill family had moved into the area in 1833 when Henry Colden Antill purchased 640 acres on the Molonglo River, towards the further reaches of the plains, for five shillings an acre. The next year,

Antill bought another 640 acres in the Primrose Valley, part of the larger Molonglo Plains, adding another 640 acres to it later in the year. He made still further purchases in the area in 1834 and 1835. An 1837 map of the region shows two extensive Antill properties near the headwaters of the Molonglo River.

It is likely that Thomas Wentworth Wills came into the world in a manager's or caretaker's hut on one of these properties. At that time, it was rough living, made rougher by a more extreme climate than Horace and Elizabeth had known in Sydney. Just two weeks before Tom was born — like his namesake uncle, the child and adult would always be known as Tom — the area was struck by a heavy blizzard which dumped ten to twelve inches of snow across the plains. Horace embraced the challenges and opportunities the Molonglo Plains offered; in late 1835 or early 1836, he purchased a 1480-acre property there. Named *Burra*, the property was located on Burra Creek, which flowed into the Molonglo River, and was around 15 kilometres from Queanbeyan. Within months, he had stocked his property with cattle and sheep he purchased from graziers around Bathurst.

Burra would not be a long-term home to the Wills family. In 1837, they moved again, this time further south to a property Horace purchased on the Murrumbidgee River between Gundagai and Tumut. No reasons have been put forward for the move, which was most likely prompted by the fact that there was little room to expand on the Molonglo Plains. Horace seems to have decided that his primary focus as a pastoralist would be on the production of fine wool, and the flocks he would need to produce this wool needed more land than was available to him at Molonglo. He sought greater pasturage to the south and moved his flocks there but, again, the new property would be just a waystation en route to something else.

* * *

Even more and sometimes better land continued to be found and opened up to settlement much further to the south and south-west of the limits of settlement in New South Wales. In 1836, Major Thomas Mitchell, the colony's Surveyor General and a keen explorer, had passed through a well-watered area that would eventually form part of the Wimmera region on his epic expedition from Sydney to the western shores of Bass Strait, hundreds of kilometres to the south. Mitchell named the region he passed through *Australia Felix* — Australia the Beautiful — but it would be known officially as the Southern District of New South Wales or, more popularly, as the Port Phillip District.

The publication of Mitchell's journal describing the potential of the land he had traversed caused a minor rush to take up land in some of the areas he had praised so generously. There were already small settlements at Melbourne and Portland, established by Van Diemonians hungry for land. Mitchell's journal caused ten times as many New South Welshmen to also look to the new district for better opportunities than those available elsewhere. One who was prepared to try his luck in the new south land was Horace's older brother, Tom Wills. Sight unseen, he purchased a large parcel of land on the Yarra River upstream from Melbourne in what would become the suburb of Kew. Then, in 1839, he overlanded from Minto to Melbourne where he purchased more land in the bustling little township as well as town lots in the new settlement at Geelong and a farm at Point Henry, just outside Geelong.

Tom Wills also wrote to his younger brother Horace, describing the opportunities the new district offered and urging him to consider them. Horace did not take too much time to come to a decision.

*　　*　　*

Horace led his own overlanding party away from the Murrumbidgee on

29 April 1840. He started out riding alongside the covered wagon which carried Elizabeth and young Tom as well as the wife and child of one of his farm labourers who had opted to accompany him. They drove with them some 5000 sheep and 500 cattle, travelling slowly along a line that pointed endlessly towards the south. Their overall speed was determined by the pace of the livestock, and as this usually varied between slow and very slow, all were prepared for a leisurely trip to wherever it was that they were headed; Horace was confident that he would recognise their destination when he saw it.

When they reached the Murray River, discovered by Europeans a decade or so earlier, it was running quite high from the winter rains which had fallen in its catchment. The stock was swum across without any major problems, and a rudimentary bridge was constructed for the wagon and drays and for those who couldn't swim. Weeks later, towards the end of the southern spring, the party crossed well-watered plains and came to rest at the base of a medium-sized mountain, an outrider to a more extensive range that lay directly across their path. They had been following the wheel ruts left by Mitchell's party five years earlier and Horace knew that the range ahead was the Grampians, named by Mitchell after another range of mountains in his native Scotland. Horace decided to call the singly mountain Mount Ararat, "for there, like the Ark, we rested".

Much of the region had already been taken up by pastoralists, many of whom were keen to sell their landholdings if the price was right. One of these was Charles Browning Hall, who was an explorer as well as a pastoralist; Hall's Gap is named after him. Hall owned several properties in the district, including most of the land around the site where the Wills' party had ended their overland journey. That property was called *Barton* and Horace purchased it soon after he arrived, sometime in early 1841. He financed the purchase by selling his cattle to another local landowner named Richard Bunbury. Bunbury had been a captain in the Royal Navy and, more recently, the first harbourmaster at Williamstown, but had moved to the Wimmera to become a pastoralist. He paid a premium price of six guineas a head for Horace's cattle.

After making some improvements at *Barton* — the party all living in tents while they did so — Horace determined that the property was too small and unsuitable in other ways to the large-scale wool operation he had envisioned. For 18 months, he negotiated with both Bunbury and Hall to put together the property that he really wanted. By December 1842, all the negotiations had been concluded. Horace sold *Barton* to Bunbury and from Hall bought three properties, runs named *Lexington, La Rose* and *Mokepilly*, the name given to the area by the local, Mount William Aboriginal tribe.

Horace consolidated the three runs into one and kept the name *Lexington* for that run. The new Lexington was shaped, broadly, like a triangle, extending from Mount Redman to Cathcart to Hall's Gap. It covered 120,000 acres (more than 50,000 hectares), large enough for even Horace's expansive dreams.

*   *   *

After selecting an appropriate home site at Lexington, Horace and his team of labourers got down to making their farm a viable farm and a showcase of what can happen when determination meets opportunity. The overlanders' tents and crude shelters they had lived in were soon replaced by split timber and bark huts and sheds, then by a comfortable homestead and outbuildings. To cater for the large numbers of sheep he was planning to run, Horace employed several additional shepherds and put them in charge of the outstations he created at Hall's Gap and on the Pomonal side of the Grampians.

Taking over such a large area of prime grazing land inevitably brought Horace into direct contact with the original occupants of the area. Europeans had called them the Mount William tribe, because that mountain was at the heart of the land, and by the time Horace took up Lexington, they were already in visible decline. During the winter months of 1841, the Port Phillip District's Protector of Aboriginal, a Mr. A. G. Robinson, visited the Grampian/Pyrenees region to try to make sense of the rapid reduction in the Aboriginal population there. He stayed with the Wills at their Barton property, and presumably Horace was given some insight into the local problems by Robinson.

There were relatively few problems in Horace's relationship with the Aboriginals that he and the other pastoralists were forcing off their traditional lands; Horace was always prepared to put up with the occasional stock loss for the sake of good relations. At one stage, Aboriginals displaced from elsewhere moved into the traditional home of the Mount William Aboriginal, tensions grew, and there were a number of inter-tribal clashes. As part of these, a hut keeper employed by Horace was murdered near Mount William. The locals urged Horace to attack the interlopers, but he was not prepared to open hostilities with either of the tribes.

He had early established a modus vivendi for working with the Mount William tribesmen. If they speared one of his sheep, he would ride out to the spot where this had occurred and fire his gun into the air. He would retreat to cover if spears were thrown, but then wait until women and children were sent to retrieve the weapons before giving them all a friendly wave and riding away. He would always kill a bullock or two for them when times were hard and would not take part in any punitive raids that some of the other settlers organised.

In the intermittent diary that Horace would keep during his years at Lexington, on 20 May 1843, he recorded, *"Yesterday Ned Kenny with a ewe flock just commenced lambing had his flock rushed by the blacks' dogs;*

one ewe killed and two young lambs. One ewe's leg broken and many bit."
Horace did narrowly escape injury in one clash around this time, but he
responded with his pen rather than with his rifle. As would become his
habit, Horace drafted a long letter to the Governor in Sydney, outlining
the various issues he and the other pastoralists in the district were facing,
and asked that a magistrate and special constables be despatched. He
also took the opportunity to criticise the practice of placing Aboriginal
reserves around areas now closely settled by Europeans.

The relationship between Horace and his farm labourers and the local
Aboriginals was generally a good one. When mutual trust had been established, Horace was more than happy to employ Aboriginals on his station
and assist them in times of hardship. In this, he had a young and effective
assistant in young Tom Wills. At Lexington, Tom quickly learned to
speak the local Aboriginal dialect and he would amuse all, Aboriginals
included, by singing their songs and imitating their dances.

*   *   *

In hindsight, the years between 1841 and 1843 were not good for the
Port Phillip District and for those attempting to establish business enterprises there. The local economy was passing through the bust phase of
a boom and bust cycle so typical of new and growing economies. That
Horace Wills of Lexington came through that period of economic flux
without any major setbacks may therefore seem to have been somewhat
fortuitous. In his periodic diary, Horace noted that, "*while the country
resounds with the complaints of capitalists, we enjoy a comparative independence...*" This comparative independence did not come about through
chance, though; Horace was proving to be both a very practical farmer
as well as an astute businessman.

Horace did, in fact, have a stroke of luck in the early days after overlanding from New South Wales. He was always going to run sheep on his property, and the 500 cattle he had overlanded with his sheep flock were something of a back-up in case things went wrong with the sheep. He sold those cattle to Richard Bunbury before the recession set in; had he arrived six months later, he would have been lucky to be paid one pound a head for them.

The six guineas a head that Bunbury paid really was a windfall. Horace also recognised that the boom/bust cycle was primarily the result of speculators and profiteering, and that, *"such a state of things would not last any man with common sense could foresee"*. Horace's response to all that speculation was to take control of those things he could control, starting with his property and what took place there.

With the consolidation of Lexington into one substantial run, Horace was able to focus on making it a model of efficiency, an agricultural testing ground for all that he had learned and considered in the past decade. Where other pastoralists bridled at the wages being demanded by farm labourers, Horace paid them without complaint. If a simple shepherd asked for one pound a week, plus keep, then that was what Horace paid. He would even ask them to think of ways to improve how the farm worked, and then listened courteously to their answers. The results that flow from such an approach soon became apparent.

Horace arrived in the Port Phillip District with a flock of 5000 sheep; within two years of consolidating Lexington, that flock had grown to 8000. Through careful animal husbandry, selective breeding and considered purchase, plus land clearance and pest eradication, the carrying capacity of Lexington continually increased. By 1846, Horace was shearing 20,000 sheep at Lexington, a figure that would grow to around 30,000 by 1850 and which was probably the upper limit of capacity. The property's wool clip also grew in proportion, from a few dozen bales in the early years to 200 or more by the end of the decade.

Over time, Horace refined almost everything about the production cycle at Lexington. In the early years there, stock losses to native and wild dogs were considerable. After some research, poisoned baits seemed to be the best way to eradicate the pest. After some research, Horace was the first pastoralist in the district to use strychnine as the bait's poison, and his success meant that others soon followed Horace's lead in this. He also found that the best dip to use on sheep before shearing commenced was one based on an infusion of tobacco leaves. To ensure a continuity of supply, Horace procured tobacco plant seeds and was able to use the tobacco he grew himself to both dip his sheep and fill his pipe.

Before shearing, Lexington's sheep would be washed and dipped — using Horace's solution — in either Mokepilly or Salt Creek. After the shearing season, bullock drays took the wool clip to Geelong for onward passage to the textile mills of northern England. Three months after they departed Lexington the bullock drays would return, carrying stores, clothing and foodstuffs purchased in Geelong and Melbourne. Horace himself would sometimes join in for part of this annual ritual and would use the opportunity it presented to indulge in two of his favourite recreations, studying the latest developments in farming, and writing long letters to the various newspapers available in the colonies.

On the subject of farming, he really did have a lot to write about. Fine wool production would remain his primary focus and Horace was forever looking for ways to make the entire process more productive and efficient. By late 1849, he had invented and perfected what he called a "Lever Box Soaking Machine," a superior way of dipping sheep, and something he described proudly in several letters he wrote to newspaper editors. He described in some detail how 60 sheep could be dipped at the same time and kept in the water for as long as was necessary. The machine was operated by levers attached to ropes and windlasses, and it required two men and an observer to operate. He noted that, if the sheep became fatigued, the platform they were on could be easily raised before any of the sheep drowned.

Nothing escaped his attention. When Horace decided to explore the possibility of adding a wheat crop to Lexington's pasturage, he decided that the quality of the seed that was planted was one of the main determinants of whether or not the crop would be successful. To this end, he trained a number of local Aboriginal women to sort and grade wheat seed. Not unsurprisingly, the experiment was a success. He planted and cultivated an orchard and a vegetable garden and experimented in other areas as well. It was at Lexington that Horace designed and constructed one of Australia's first commercially viable wool presses. It was also at Lexington that Horace learned of the development of fencing wire in Europe and ordered 50 miles (80 kilometres) of it — at two and sixpence a yard — from a manufacturer in Austria.

Horace was also conscious that he was part of a wider, pioneering community. When a gang of bushrangers raided several properties in the district, Horace was one of the first to join the posse which was formed to try to track them down, a decision that could have cost him his life. That posse had been unsuccessful in its pursuit but just a couple of weeks later, a group of ruffians rode up to the Lexington homestead early one morning. Reining their horses in outside the house, a number of them began shouting, "Shoot him! Burn him out!"

Horace suspected that the group of horsemen were part or all of the bushranging gang that he had so recently been chasing and he also suspected that they may have arrived seeking revenge. He was also keenly aware that his wife and children were in the house. When there was a pounding on the front door, Horace opened it to face the men, alone and unarmed. He then spoke to the man who appeared to be in charge, firstly asking him to calm down one of his companions, who was continuing to scream abuse. Horace said that courtesy and manners he had learned young compelled him to offer travellers — such as these men who had obviously ridden long and hard — such hospitality as he was able to offer, and promptly invited them all in for breakfast.

After he had fed them all, the men took their leave and rode away from Lexington without doing any damage to Horace's person or property. Before they left, the leader took Horace aside and admitted that their original plan had been to simply call Horace out and then shoot him. His manly bearing and his willing ness to share convinced them to do otherwise.

*   *   *

Lexington was partly about agriculture and horticulture, and how the application of hard work and scientific principles could bring about increased yields and increased rewards. But it was also about family, and about how success in business, whatever business that may be, was only significant if it brought a better life to those important to the man who was successful. Horace hinted at some of the dimensions of this in a couple of diary entries. In one, he recorded that, *"Here I must bear testimony to the unrepining devotion and uninterrupted affection of my partner... She has been the star of my destiny. From a wild youth, she has centred my affections on the domestic hearth."*

While living at Lexington, Horace and Elizabeth had another five children; two daughters they named Sarah and Emily, and three sons, Cedric, Horace and Egbert. Their births spurred another entry in Horace's diary; he spoke of he and Elizabeth, *"congratulating ourselves on the probability of providing a good education for our children and leaving them the fruits of our frugality and industry"*.

Horace was painfully aware of his own educational limitations, and he remained a lifelong advocate of self-education, especially in the areas of literature and science. He and Elizabeth gave their children their first school lessons at Lexington and used visits to and from neighbours as educational as well as social opportunities. Both parents believed that their children's' future success would depend on more than just home schooling though, and in 1847 Tom Wills was sent as a boarder to what Horace referred to as the "Brickworks Seminary" in Melbourne. It was to be a preparatory school for Tom who, in early 1850, departed Melbourne for England where he would attend Rugby School. His holidays and extra-curricular activities would be attended to by his aunt and uncle, William and Sarah Redfern, by then resident in London.

*   *   *

As the years passed at Lexington, the tents and huts that had sufficed in the early days were replaced by wooden and stone cottages, and then by a more substantial homestead and outbuildings. Although by then the various colonies were self-sufficient in many things, the pastoralists still looked to England for many of the finer things in life. In the late 1840's, one consignment of goods despatched to Lexington by Horace's London agent contained the following:

> *3 barrels Roman cement; 5 puncheons glass and earthenware; four quart decanters and four pint decanters valued at 56 pounds; a case of plate, value 55 pounds; silver plate, value 84 pounds; one case of books and one case of globes; cottage piano; floor cloths and rugs; case of perfumery; and 10 hogsheads of stout.*

Most of these items were for the grand homestead Horace planned to build to celebrate a decade of occupancy at Lexington. Taking well over a year to construct, the home was built used timber trimmed in Lexington's timber mill and bricks made on the property. When completed, the building, its fittings and furnishings, attracted favourable comment from all who visited, one noting the, "*shining oil-cloth on the table and damask covering on the chairs*". Horace's favourite room was the library, which he described in his diary as, "*...furnished with terrestrial and celestial globes and maps, instruments of native warfare....an excellent collection of books.... and my double barrel gun and pistol carbine, old friends from Sydney*".

Flanked by storehouses, accommodation for farm workers and offices, the new home was large and comfortable, and its two-metre-deep cellar was large enough to keep a lot of food and drink cool in even the hottest summer. That building would still be there a century later, but the Wills' occupancy of it would only be brief. They moved into it in August 1852 and within a few months, Horace was looking to move out again.

*   *   *

The problem was that Victoria, by then a colony in its own right, had been found to contain some of the richest goldfields in the world. They attracted hundreds, then thousands of Australian gold seekers as well, stripping towns of most of their able-bodied men and attracting farm labourers and shepherds like a magnet. Slowly, but inevitably, Horace lost most of his Lexington workforce. For a while, he replaced them with Chinese workers, but they resigned en masse after a dispute with Tom Baker, the overseer. The Chinese simply walked away, taking the cook with them.

In October 1852, Horace sold Lexington, with its 29,000 sheep and 3000 cattle, to a Mr. Pynsent for thirty-five thousand pounds. Soon afterwards, their belongings safely packed aboard a line of bullock drays and covered wagons, Horace Wills again led his family south. Another opportunity and another adventure beckoned.

THE BUNYIP ARISTOCRACY

fter a leisurely overland journey that occupied several weeks, Horace re-established his family at a property he named *Belle Vue*, located on the Point Henry peninsula just to the south of the thriving Victorian regional centre of Geelong. Like most of the decisions that Horace made, this one was based on a careful appraisal of all relevant issues. Several factors impelled Horace to resettle where he did. He already knew the area reasonably well; the wool from Lexington had been exported through the port of Geelong, and it was also where Horace had personally bought many of the supplies and fittings for Lexington.

There were personal, family reasons as well. The 304 acres Horace bought in the Moolap subdivision of Point Henry was almost adjacent to a property purchased by his brother Thomas over a decade earlier. As important in Horace's reckoning was the fact that Elizabeth's sister, Catherine, now lived in Geelong. Catherine had married a Sydney merchant named William Roope and they, too, had lived in the Molonglo/Limestone Plains area before overlanding to the Port Phillip District several years earlier. If nothing else, moving to Point Henry would promote the kind of social and family life that had simply not been available at Lexington.

The party that overlanded to Belle Vue comprised Horace and Elizabeth and their children; the Lexington overseer, Tom Baker, and his wife and their several children; and their best shepherd from Lexington, an older man named Ned Kenny. They had all known each other for several years and now the journey from Lexington was like a refresher camp for pioneers. When they arrived at Pont Henry, they pitched their tents, set up a kitchen and built holding pens for the stock they would purchase to turn their open paddocks into a productive farm. It was April 1853 when they arrived; they would have to live through a southern winter in their tents. It wouldn't be easy, especially for the children, but Horace was confident it would be the last time he would put them all through it.

*   *   *

Horace Wills, as he entered his middle years, retained a strong sense of his own capacity to learn and grow. The 304 acres of *Belle Vue* would have fitted comfortable into any one of his larger paddocks at Lexington, so he would not even attempt the large-scale wool production that had been so successful there. Instead, he would focus on agricultural and horticultural quality across a range of farming disciplines. Horace was also mindful that he was only part of a much larger Australian enterprise, that of increasing the various colonies' self-sufficiency, and so he was always prepared to share his growing expertise with others.

In fact, rather than becoming just a passive sharer of knowledge, Horace became an active promoter of agricultural excellence. He was the driving force behind the formation of the Geelong and Western District Agricultural and Horticultural Society in February 1955. He served as the Society's president for several tears after its formation. That year, the Society also sponsored the first ever Geelong Show, at which Horace was the official judge of both the sheep and agricultural implements competition. That year, Horace also became patron of Geelong's first orphanage, perhaps recalling the family experiences that he and Elizabeth shared. William Roope agreed to sit on the orphanage's board of trustees.

Horace also seemed determined to make Belle Vue a living, working example of his theories and practices; he was successful in that as well. Always an avid correspondent, Horace wrote to the editor of the Melbourne *Argus* in early September 1855 addressing the problem of wireworm and potato grub. He detailed how he had established three potato patches, one of five acres and the other two of one acre each. He treated all three in different ways, and the one where he also grew maize among the potatoes escaped the twin ravages of worm and grub.

In October 1855, Horace was awarded a prize by the Agricultural and Horticultural Society as a Gala Exhibition for one of his inventions, a subsoil pulveriser. Fifteen months later, Horace hosted a trial of threshing machines at his Belle Vue property. It was one of those rare occasions when something Horace organised was less than successful. Planned as a competition between the various types of threshing machines then available, it literally did not get off the ground because all the local machines invited to compete were being used for cropping. Horace attempted to salvage something by giving a demonstration of his own threshing machine, but it broke down.

In January 1858, Major General Macarthur's Gold Medal for the best field of wheat of not less than 20 acres was unanimously awarded to Horace for one of his wheat fields at Belle Vue. In a letter that was reprinted in several colonial newspapers, Horace attributed his gold medal wheat to a combination of his 20 years' experience, his subsoil pulveriser and a light manuring of the crop. He could have added that his continuing success as a farmer came about at a time in his life when agricultural pursuits were no longer the prime motivator of his efforts.

*   *   *

201

Democracy would come slowly and carefully to the Australian colonies, arriving in fits and starts, and promoted by a general feeling of Australianness as well as specific occurrences like the massive influx of gold-seekers in the early 1850s. Many of those gold-seekers were from Europe, where memories of the 1848 revolutions still lingered, and from the United States, where democratic principles had been validated by a revolution in the previous century. In the Colony of Victoria, the beginning of representative government arrived in 1854 when elections for a Legislative Council were announced. Either at the prompting of other pastoralists — the franchise was limited to men of means — or on the basis of his own desires, Horace decided to run for office.

The seat Horace contested was that of South Grant, and it encompassed Geelong and spread across the Bellarine Peninsula and out into the Western District. He had only one opponent; an actor and theatrical entrepreneur named Henry Deering. When the votes were counted, Horace was declared the victor, by a margin of 202 votes to 113. He would be returned to office in the 1856 elections, but Horace struggled to have the impact in politics that he had already made in agriculture.

It is possible that a political life was not what Horace had expected it would be; he was a good talker, perhaps a better writer but above all, he was a doer, and this aspect of his life may have been frustrated in the Legislative Council. He did make a mark in politics, but it was a little mark, easily overlooked in the great debates of the day. While at Lexington, Horace had joined the Portland and Geelong Immigration Society, maintaining his membership after moving to Belle Vue, and writing and speaking on the subject as a member of the Council.

In one of his periodic letters to the editor of the Melbourne *Argus* — this one penned in September 1857 — Horace explained that he had recently voted against a poll tax on Chinese emigrants, not because he was not in favour of such emigration, but because of the way the bill was worded, as it suggested that unlimited numbers of Chinese could come to Victoria provided a tax was paid upon arrival. He noted that, "*in common with most of my race, I think we already have rather more than enough of these Eversonian 'rice-eating, opium-smoking Mongolians'*".

That, and an 1858 letter about the high cost of labour making it cheaper to import foodstuffs than to produce them locally, remain Horace's major recorded contributions to the political process. In early 1859, he announced both personally and in print, that he would not be seeking re-election for a third term in 1860. Other matters were calling to him and he would answer those calls, both within Australia and overseas.

*   *   *

On 24 March 1859, through the pages of the *Argus*, Horace Wills announced to the world that he would be sailing to England aboard the steamer *Result*, and would be departing Victoria one week hence, on 31 March. Although there was no indication in the newspaper article of what the purpose of the journey might be, Horace had two clear reasons for the trip. The first was to enrol his three younger sons — Cedric, Horace and Egbert — all born at Lexington, in a suitable public school. The second was to study the latest advances in agricultural machinery.

The importance of education was something that was central to Horace's plans for his sons' futures. While his daughters would follow the fashion of the time and be educated at home by governesses and tutors, his sons required a better and broader education that that. The Wills were now part of what was being called the Bunyip Aristocracy, the cohort of primarily Australian-born businessmen and pastoralists moving towards the top of the social table through their own efforts rather than through family connections. Hard work and education were, and would remain, critical to that advancement in the Australian colonies.

The educational experiment which saw young Tom Wills attend Rugby School had been only a limited success. The Redferns reported that Tom did not seem to be giving all his attention to his academic studies, and Horace devoted most of his letters to Tom in exhortations to his son not to waste his time and opportunities, and to make some effort to at least improve the quality of his handwriting. Tom was and would remain an academic plodder, but he did develop into an outstanding sportsman, competing successfully in rugby football itself but even more so at cricket.

It was the sporting arena which continued to attract Tom following his return to Victoria in 1854. While Horace was doing whatever he could to help Tom establish himself as a lawyer, Tom himself was blazing like a comet across the colony's sporting firmament. He would both represent and captain Victoria's cricket team and play the game for most of the leading local teams. He would also be the sporting brains brain behind a small volunteer committee which drew up the rules for a new football code that would in time become the largest and most popular in Australia. Away from the sports field, though, Tom Wills struggled. He seemed disinterested in office work, but always made himself available to travel and play either football or cricket.

Horace would not make the same mistake with his other sons. After some thorough research, Horace settled on Dr. Pilgrim's School in Bonn, Germany, as the most appropriate institute of learning for Cedric, Horace and Egbert, and after disembarking in London where he caught up with the Redferns, he took his sons across the Channel and then across Europe to Bonn where the boys were successfully enrolled in Dr. Pilgrim's School.

Back in England, he toured the countryside where he noted the various farming techniques for similar crops, and also made time to visit manufacturers of farm implements and machinery to view and discuss developments in those areas as well. He was especially taken by a traction engine, a borer, a new style of threshing machine and a portable mill. Horace also travelled to Ireland, where he visited most of the tourist attractions and, back in England once again, he negotiated with the manufacturer and gained the agency to sell the traction engine throughout the colony of Victoria. His head full of ideas and his trunk full of print material, Horace sailed for Australia, expecting to arrive back home in early 1860.

*   *   *

It was almost serendipitous. Shortly after Horace returned to Belle Vue in March 1860, he met with a new neighbour, another pastoralist named John Macdonald. John and his brother Peter had migrated to Australia from South Africa and, while John had been happy to settle as a farmer in Victoria, Peter Macdonald had joined a minor gold rush which had started in Central Queensland. He had failed to make his fortune from gold-mining but stayed on in the area to explore pastoral opportunities inland from the Rockhampton and Keppel Bay area. He was particularly taken by the potential of a property he had named *Cullinlaringo*, which meant "that which was sought and then found", in the local Aboriginal dialect.

Horace learned that Cullinlaringo was around 350 kilometres inland from the coast, near the Nogoa River, one of the tributaries of the Fitzroy. It bordered the previous limit of settlement, Rainworth Station, owned by a pastoralist named James Gregson. The nearest settlement of note was Rockhampton, itself on the Fitzroy River some 40 kilometres inland from the coast. Peter Macdonald was confident that the rich soil of the thousands of acres which comprised Cullinlaringo would support all forms of agriculture and horticulture that he bought the property on speculation. His descriptions of the land, given to Horace by John Macdonald, were so compelling that Horace decided to follow them up.

Horace had achieved all that he hoped to achieve at Belle Vue and in Victoria, and at the conclusion of his several discussions with John Macdonald, he had almost made up his mind. If suitable land was available in Central Queensland, he would relocate there and start a farm from scratch again.

Horace determined to visit the area as soon as possible and John Macdonald agreed to accompany him. They set off almost as soon as passage could be arranged, sailing firstly to Sydney where Horace was able to catch up in person with a number of relatives he had not seen in many years. He also took the opportunity to purchase a revolver and to have his old shotgun repaired. From Sydney, the two men again sailed on a steamship to Rockhampton on the Fitzroy River. That voyage took them nine days which was two days longer than the usual voyage.

Either during the voyage or after they arrived in Rockhampton, Horace was told that, in Central Queensland, there seemed to be a state of perpetual warfare between the European settlers and the various tribes who inhabited the area. Shortly after their arrival and while out looking for some hired horses which had strayed from their campsite, Horace spotted a group of Aboriginals moving through the bush in his direction. He was unarmed, but quickly found a hiding spot. He learned later that the band he had spotted was actually a group of Native Police, out of uniform and heading into the bush to go hunting.

After a rugged and trying overland journey, probably guided by Peter Macdonald, Horace Wills' little party reached Cullinlaringo, a place Horace would subsequently describe as, *"the prettiest country I have ever seen"*. It was certainly frontier country as well. In the countryside all around Cullinlaringo were bands of Aboriginal, some of whom seemed to have never seen a European or a horse before. Cullinlaringo was all that Horace had hoped it would be, and more. After an almost perfunctory inspection, Horace made an offer for the property, which Peter

Macdonald accepted, and for 2100 pounds Cullinlaringo became the latest Wills property.

The deal agreed, Horace and John Macdonald began their long journey back to Geelong. At Brisbane, Horace engaged a local agent and arranged for the purchase of a flock of sheep he would later use to stock Cullinlaringo. He decided that 6000 ewes and wethers, quality stock from the Darling Downs, would form the basis of a much larger flock that would be driven overland to Cullinlaringo, and issued the appropriate authorisations. As he left Brisbane on a steamer south, Horace thought he might have to make yet another trip north to finalise a number of plans that he was now hatching.

*   *   *

There was a blur of activity back at Belle Vue. By now, Horace seems to have pretty much lost patience with his oldest son. While he was a proud father when it came to Tom's success as a cricketer and a footballer, he was a practical father when it came to understanding what success really was. Tom's attempts to become a lawyer, to become a professional of any stamp, had not led anywhere so Horace decided to take him to Cullinlaringo to try to make a farmer of him.

With this as the ultimate objective, Horace first organised for Tom to work at a blacksmith's shop on the Queenscliff Road, not far from Belle Vue. After learning a range of skills there, Horace had also arranged for Tom to spend time learning the practical aspects of farming at a property further out towards the Western District, Barrigal Farm, near Skipton. The farm was owned and run by Alec Anderson, an old friend of Horace's from his days at Lexington. For a time while he worked there, Tom was engaged to one of Anderson's daughters, an engagement broken off by one father with the approval of the other.

Horace was absent for much of Tom's apprenticeship. In September 1860, he again travelled to Queensland to purchase additional stock and to also reconnoitre and plan the various stages of their major overland trip from southern to central Queensland. The trip included a series of unexpected encounters. In Sydney, Horace met an old school friend he had not seen for 35 years, and on the Darling Downs he met a station manager who had been at Rugby with Tom. While out on the Downs, he bought another 4000 sheep and arranged for the newly enlarged flock to be assembled in early 1861, when he planned to return to begin the trek north to Cullinlaringo.

On his way back to Geelong, Horace stopped in Sydney for several days. There, he ordered and paid for four strong bullock drays, tarpaulins and eleven tents, all to be ready for collection in early 1861. While he was doing all this, Alec Anderson — who had also agreed to act as Horace's agent in Geelong — had signed on a number of workmen to join Horace's overlanding party to Cullinlaringo. Among them were two stockmen named Henry Reid and John Moore, both regarded as being at or near the top of their trade.

By the time Horace returned home to Belle Vue, Tom Wills had learned to shoe a horse and shear a sheep. In fact, as he proudly pointed out to his father, he had actually sheared 30 sheep in his first full day as a shearer.

*   *   *

Despite Horace's capacity for hard work and planning, it was probably all a bit rushed towards the end. Among the many organisational matters in the final few weeks were the putting together of the travelling party and the final purchases of stock. The sheep he had already bought, and those he further intended to buy on the Darling Downs were ewes and wethers, but to improve the future flocks at Cullinlaringo, Horace purchased over 100 prime rams from breeders around the Bellarine Peninsula. The rams would travel by steamship to Brisbane with the rest of the overlanding party, and they would set out from there for Cullinlaringo sometime in January 1861; Horace expected to arrive at his new home in August.

All along, it had been agreed that Elizabeth and their daughters would remain at Belle Vue until Cullinlaringo was sufficiently developed for them to relocate there. Dropping them all on a distant, sub-tropical frontier and expecting them to live in tents again for months on end was something that neither Horace nor Elizabeth would now countenance. Even without his family, the overlanding party was a substantial enterprise and Horace knew that taking it safely to Cullinlaringo would occupy all his waking moments. Two of his original workers from Lexington would again accompany Horace: his overseer, Tom Baker, and his senior shepherd, Ned Kenny. Quite late in the planning process, it was agreed that Baker's wife and their children would join the party. Two of those children were adult sons, James and David.

Also leaving Belle Vue with the overlanding party would be a senior station hand, Patrick Manion, his wife and their young family. The others who would make the trip from Geelong were primarily farm labourers who had been contacted and contracted by Alec Anderson while Horace was away on his second trip to Queensland. They included bullock drivers, shepherds, farm labourers and bushmen, some of whom had already worked seasonally at Belle Vue. There were men named Pickering and Wheedon, alongside seasoned veterans like John Moore and Henry Reid. One of the stockmen was George Elliott, a local sportsman whose brother was the wicketkeeper in Tom Wills' Victorian cricket team.

They were all ready to go early in the new year of 1861. On 8 January, Horace wrote a final letter from Belle Vue to his three sons in Germany. In it, he related how Peter Macdonald had seen some Aboriginals near

Cullinlaringo, and that they had been very kind to Macdonald and his party. He also mentioned that his party would be taking all the guns, *"even the little one"*.

THE OVERLANDERS

O n Sunday 3 February 1861, the steamship *Telegraph* of 700 tons, sailed into Moreton Bay and a short distance up the Brisbane River to its anchorage. The *Telegraph* had departed Sydney on 23 January with a mixed cargo and a large number of passengers. Many of those passengers made up the Wills Overlanding Party and within hours, and for a short time only, they were the toast of Brisbane Town.

In the days that followed, Brisbane's largest newspaper, the *Courier*, published and republished quite an expansive article on the Wills Overlanding Party, its makeup and its intentions. It described both Horace and Tom as "well-known enterprising gentlemen from Victoria". Tom was noted as having an Australia-wide reputation due to his exploits as captain of the Victorian cricket team, while Horace was described as, "a squatter of large experience in Victoria".

The Wills Overlanding Party was described as comprising around 20 men, women and children, four drays and 111 superior rams. Special mention was made of the large number of dogs travelling with the over-landers, especially the five half-breed bloodhounds the Wills had brought to protect the party. The *Courier's* article ended with the observation that the Wills Overlanding Party would leave Brisbane for the Darling Downs, where it would collect some 10,000 sheep that Horace Wills had purchased several months earlier. The party would be overlanding those sheep, and their other stock, to what the paper referred to as "Mulgoa Station", 200 miles inland from Rockhampton.

Wills and the party departed Brisbane at the end of that first week of February. Just a few days later, and while still en route to collect their sheep on the Darling Downs, tragedy struck. At around 5 p.m. on the afternoon of Monday 18 February, after the day's travel had been completed and the stock all safely penned, two of the stockmen, Henry Reid and George Lynn, decided to cool off by for a swim in the nearby Lockyer Creek. Shortly after the men entered the water, Reid complained about the amount of timber scattered across the floor of the creek. George Lynn, who had swum away from Reid, said that the deeper water seemed to be free of snags.

Reid began to paddle across to where Lynn was splashing about in a large pool when he was suddenly caught up in the flow of the creek. Lynn grabbed Reid by the chin as he drifted past, but Reid's response was to seize the other man and they both sank below the surface. The noise the men had made attracted others to the unfolding drama. One of the shepherds, an older man named John Moore, arrived just as Lynn called, "Look out!", and both men slipped beneath the water. Moore dived in and was able to grab Reid underwater by his hair, but the strength of the creek's current forced him to let go of the bullock driver. Lynn had made it back to the surface and now made several unsuccessful dives into the water looking for his friend.

The local police were soon involved in the attempt to recover Henry Reid's body. One of them put a series of stakes across the creek and the following day, Reid's body snagged on one of these. An inquest held at Gatton on 22 February heard evidence from all those who had been near Reid at the time of his death; the Coroner recorded a finding of accidental death by drowning.

*   *   *

Horace Wills' original prediction would be proven wrong; it would take a full ten months for his party to travel from Belle Vue to their new station at Cullinlaringo. Early in the journey, as if in recompense for the loss of Henry Reid, overseer Tom Baker's wife gave birth to a baby daughter around 25 March. Mother and child were both well, with Horace acting as a doctor for the birth. Soon afterwards, station hand Patrick Manion and his wife also welcomed a baby daughter, Horace again taking responsibility for the delivery. Even young Tom Wills grew out of the semi-permanent depression which had afflicted him since he learned he would be leaving Victoria. He and James Baker, the overseer's oldest son, grew close to one another on the overland trip, Tom teaching the younger man how to load and fire a revolver as they travelled.

After almost eight months on the road, Horace Wills and his party were in Central Queensland, approaching Cullinlaringo. One of the reasons for their slow rate of progress was beyond their control. Winter and spring had been mild but wet that year, with heavy rains causing floods at several points on their proposed line of march. Days and then weeks were lost waiting for floodwaters to recede or seeking alternative routes north. The sheer logistics of the trip also guaranteed delays. Ewes fell pregnant or ill, and some flocks moved faster than others, just as some shepherds were better organised than others.

The final few weeks travel to Cullinlaringo was actually undertaken by two separate parties. The main party was led by Horace and comprised most of the drays and wagons, plus a small portion of the flock. Around 70 kilometres behind them, Tom Baker, three shepherds and several farm labourers drove the main flock, primarily ewes and young lambs, along the trail blazed by Horace. Their leader's excitement was, by now, palpable.

On 28 September 1861, the *Rockhampton Bulletin and Central Queensland Advertiser* published a letter penned by Horace arguing the pastoralists' case for a punt to be established at a crossing point on the lower Dawson River. Back in almost civilised country, he dashed off several other letters as well, seeking shepherds for his new run at Cullinlaringo and ordering supplies and equipment for the main homestead and outbuildings he intended to construct there. Like the call for shepherds, the orders for supplies and equipment was directed to Rockhampton, with Horace instructing that all hardware that he ordered was to be delivered to the Albinia Downs station, and he would organise for its collection from there.

The boundary between the Cullinlaringo and Rainworth Stations — the aptly-named Separation Creek — was crossed in early October. About five kilometres past the creek, Horace found another lovely little creek running off to the west. Close to that creek, on a piece of high ground that was both flat and relatively clear, Horace selected the site for his future homestead. To the south of the site, and no more than two kilometres away, a range of hills rose out of the plains and marched away majestically to the west. The little creek which so attracted Horace meandered down a shallow valley as far as the eye could see, its banks protected by ti tree and paperbark. To the east, the ranges stretched around the property like a horseshoe, while a rocky plain started at the homestead paddock and continued off into the distance to the north. Looking all around from the centre of the site, Horace could see undulating country which was well-covered by grass.

*   *   *

Work commenced on the homestead complex almost immediately. In the centre of the chosen area, a circle of tents to be occupied by the women and children was erected, their placement being determined by safety and security considerations. Beyond these, the workmen's tents were erected and work also began almost immediately on the construction of storage huts and sheep pens. These pens were formed by light brush fences, and several men were detailed to this task. A large area was also fenced and cleared near where the main house would be built. Intended as a future vegetable patch, the children were allowed to join in turning over the soil and planting the seeds.

On 3 August 1861, as Wills and his party were approaching Central Queensland, the Rockhampton *Bulletin* publishes an article under the headline, "The Blacks."

> *"Reports have reached town," it read, "that the blacks for some time past caused much annoyance and loss of settlers at Waverley, Studleigh, and at Anelow's Station in the vicinity of Broadwater by spearing a large number of cattle. The police are in search of them but have as yet been unsuccessful, owing to the difficulty of tracking them though the mangrove swamp. A party who recently started from Waverley in search of the blacks met with a quantity of spears, nullah-nullahs and other warlike implements."*

Four years earlier, in October 1857, the Fraser family homestead on the lower Dawson River, *Hornet Bank*, had been subject to a coordinated attack by the Aboriginal tribe they had displaced, the Yeeman. Striking without warning, the attackers killed eleven Europeans, including most of the Fraser children. The colonists' retribution was terrible, with reports of up to 300 Yeeman men, women and children being shot down, not because of any involvement they may have had in the *Hornet Bank* killings, but simply because they were Yeeman.

Horace Wills was no fool. During his previous visit to Cullinlaringo, he had listened to and learned from the European pastoralists who had opened up the rich countryside inland from Rockhampton, and he was a prodigious reader of local newspapers. He was well-aware of the fraught relationship between Aboriginals and Europeans and took what he considered to be the appropriate precautions. As he had written in the letter to his sons in Germany, Wills' party was very heavily armed. It carried rifles, shotguns and revolvers and Horace's tent, part of the inner circle, also serving as an armoury. The firearms stored there were cleaned and oiled and were kept loaded and ready for action. From the day they arrived at Cullinlaringo, Horace had implemented a 24-hour system of sentinels as well.

On either the day that Horace and his advance party arrived at Cullinlaringo, or more probably the next day, the bustling little campsite was visited by a troop of Native Police under the command of a Lieutenant Patrick. It is not known what information, if any, was passed by one party to the other as no records of the meeting were kept. One story, if it was known to either Patrick or Wills, would certainly have been passed, if known, because of its crucial significance. A short time previously, a few days perhaps, but certainly no longer than two weeks, a number of wandering sheep had been caught, and several killed, by a small band of Aboriginal. No location was given, but it was most likely that this took place on Rainworth Station, not far from Cullinlaringo.

While still in possession of several of the sheep, the Aboriginals were found by a troop of Native Police who were accompanied by two white men. There were no discussions, no explanations offered for acceptance or rejection; the police party simply opened fire, killing two Aboriginals on the spot and scattering all the others. According to the laws which guided those Aboriginal, the killing of the warriors had to be avenged. If the actual killers could not be found, revenge could be directed against other members of their tribe i.e. other Europeans.

*   *   *

Just a few days after the party arrived at Cullinlaringo, a package of newspapers sent via Brisbane and Rockhampton arrived with one of the labourers Horace had contracted from that town. In one of the editions of one of the Geelong newspapers, Horace learned that he had become a father again. Elizabeth, who had been barely pregnant when he departed Belle Vue, had given birth to a daughter. Mother and daughter were reportedly doing well.

*   *   *

Shortly after work began on the construction of the sheep pens, Horace had his first encounter with the local Aboriginal. While riding along the edge of a timbered area, he startled a young Aboriginal woman carrying a baby. Making what he hoped would be seen as peaceful signs, he carefully dismounted and, smiling, put a silk handkerchief on the baby's head as a bonnet. Just a few days later, a small party of Aboriginals appeared at the Wills' homestead camp. Horace welcomed them and arranged for them all to receive a small token gift. The group returned the following day with some additional numbers, and within a week quite a large encampment of Aboriginals appeared at the base of the hills around two kilometres from the homestead camp.

When that cam appeared, Horace put in place a policy of quite deliberate contact with those who lived there. Initially, several sheep were slaughtered, and their carcases presented to the Aboriginals as a gesture of friendship. A small flock of sheep was then drafted off from the main flock, and the Aboriginals were given to understand that the animals were theirs for the taking and that replacements would be provided when the first lot had been consumed. Parties of Aboriginals visiting the homestead camp were presented with packages of tobacco, sugar and flour. Shepherds and station hands were cautioned against doing anything which might antagonise the Aboriginal.

This approach flew in the face of all the advice Horace had been given about dealing with the Aboriginals of Central Queensland. Keep them at a distance, he was told, and do not allow them into your campsite under any circumstances. Horace had heard the tales of killings and revenge, of petty theft and grand theft, and decided to trust his own experience and his own beliefs in how to deal with people. A decade or more on the frontier had taught Horace many things, but that frontier had been a long, long way to the south.

Horace's policy of non-confrontation and co-operation appeared to be paying off, in the short term at least. The Aboriginals themselves began bringing gifts of kangaroo and other game they had killed to the homestead camp, and some of their women and children became favourites with the European children. Several individual shepherds from the camp who became lost on the outer edges of the run were escorted back to the homestead camp by bands of armed Aboriginals who had found them wandering in the bush. The Aboriginals who came into Wills' camp were never carrying weapons, and gradually the Europeans came to accept their presence there as normal.

As the policy seemed to be working, security around the homestead camp was gradually relaxed. The 24-hour sentry system introduced by Horace was cut back to an overnight guard only, and he also allowed the workmen who were away from the camp during the day to decide for themselves whether or not they carried firearms with them as they worked.

All eventually chose not to do so, as the bulky and heavy weapons reduced their ability to work in the sub-tropical heat. Horace consistently reinforced to the Aboriginals that they were not to interfere with the men as they worked and, to those men, that there were plenty of weapons in his tent and, should they ever feel vulnerable, they should arm themselves immediately.

Within just two weeks of arriving at Cullinlaringo, Horace had his team working together and working well. As a concession to the increasing heat, he had decreed that they all take a siesta for an hour or two during the early afternoon, when the sun was at its fiercest. Each morning, the shepherds would take their flocks out to a predetermined part of the run, returning in the late afternoon to put the sheep into the temporary enclosures they had prepared. Work had begun on permanent stockyards and Horace was about to send a team to collect the supplies and equipment that had been sent to Rainworth Station. Included in that load were things the men would need to construct the permanent buildings Horace had planned for Cullinlaringo. Christmas was barely two months away now, and Horace hoped that it would be his last Christmas under canvas, and his last Christmas away from his family as well.

ATTACK AND RETRIBUTION

On Sunday, 17 October 1861, Tom Wills, James Baker and Billy Albery were all up early, breakfasting and making preparations to depart around mid-morning for Albinia Downs to collect the supplies waiting for them there. Horace had outlined what he expected of them the previous day and then given them responsibility for making it happen. He had chosen the men carefully. Tom had remained something of a fish out of water; his sporting skills were not required, and he didn't seem inclined to take the lead in any of the building or farming activities that were happening all around him. His were, therefore, one set of hands that would probably not be missed. He and James Baker had remained good friends, and would therefore be company for each other, while Billy Albery was an experienced bullock driver and bushman who had been with the party since it was formed at Belle Vue.

Albery had gone off early to yoke his team to their dray, and when he returned to the homestead campsite, he was still clearly amused by something which had occurred. Just after he had yoked the team, he told the others as they gathered around, he had been surrounded by about 50 Aboriginals. Albery was uncertain about what this presaged and became concerned that something may be amiss when several warriors approached him. Those warriors then began to pummel him with the sides of their hands, almost like a stockman ascertaining the condition of livestock.

Albery was ticklish and very shortly the pummelling caused him to break into helpless laughter. The Aboriginals soon joined in and, within a few minutes, a large group of adult males were rolling around, slapping one another, and laughing uproariously. Horace and most of the others listening to Albery's tale put the story down to simple curiosity by people who had very limited experience with Europeans, and confirmed to Horace that he had little, if anything, to fear from the local Aboriginal.

Tom Wills, however, read something else into the incident. Before he left with the others to collect the supplies, Tom urged all the men at the camp to carry weapons as he felt something wasn't quite right. Horace dismissed his son's sense of foreboding as simply "boyish fears and fancy" . He did, however, accept the loan of Tom's revolver as his own was broken.

*   *   *

Tom departed on horseback, the others walking alongside the bullocks and dray. Not long after they left the campsite and soon after they crossed the creek well below the homestead, the three men came across Tom Baker, his son David and one of the shepherds travelling along slowly with a flock of lambs and ewes. Tom told the Bakers that there were now many Aboriginals around their main camp and urged the men to be careful. In the preceding weeks, and at the homestead campsite, Tom had occasionally shot one of the scavenger birds that always seemed to be circling, in part to impress the Aboriginals with the capabilities of the European's weapons. David Baker now took a leaf out of Tom's book. He took out and test-fired his rifle, hitting a small target he had set up; *"That's good enough for them,"* he said.

*   *   *

Again, sometime after Tom and his two companions departed for Albinia Downs, a large party of Aboriginals paid what Horace took to be a social call on the homestead camp. It was probably the same group who had entertained Albery a short time earlier, and they departed the camp with as little fanfare as that which accompanied their arrival. Later on, in the early afternoon when most of the Europeans were asleep or resting during the siesta, Aboriginal men entered the camp in small numbers, groups of two or three or four who moved with purpose to prearranged positions. A signal was given, and the attack commenced.....

*   *   *

Shepherd John Moore's crude hut was around 200 metres from the circle of tents the core of the homestead camp. It was stuffy at the best of times and on that Sunday, Moore found it far too hot to sleep inside, so he found a suitable tree nearby and went to sleep in its shade. He was suddenly awakened by the sound of Aboriginals calling out loudly and excitedly. Looking across to the main campsite, he saw a mob of Aboriginals — Moore would later estimate their number at 300 — overrunning the camp.

As he looked, everything slowly came into focus. Some distance away, near the front of one of the tents, Moore saw a white woman being attacked by several Aboriginals wielding war clubs. He recognised the woman as Mrs. Baker, the overseer's wife, and she soon fell to the ground beneath a flurry of blows. He now realised that there were screams and shouts coming from all over the campsite, and he heard, too, the dull thud of war clubs hitting home. In the midst of these terrible sights and sounds, Moore heard a single gunshot ring out. Looking to see where it had come from would have meant exposing himself, and Moore was not prepared to take the risk that doing so would entail.

Realising that any attempt to intervene would certainly cost his life, Moore looked around for some way to escape. There was a dry creek bed not far from where he lay in the grass and this seemed to offer the best chance for survival. To get to that creek bed though, Moore would have to cross a large patch of open ground. Fortunately for him, a small flock of sheep chose that moment to cross that open ground, moving from one patch of grassland towards another. Moore, crawling on all fours, eased his way in among the sheep and, using them as cover, was able to gain the safety of the creek.

There, Moore found a small, covered spot that he thought would provide adequate cover and protection. After a while, the sounds of violence from the campsite ended and sometime later, all sounds from the camp ceased altogether. Still, Moore sat and waited. An hour later, perhaps longer, he heard some noises coming from a different direction. Looking carefully, Moore saw that it was another flock of sheep and, moreover, that the flock was being driven by one of the shepherds, Ned Kenny from Lexington.

*　　*　　*

To Ned, it had been just another day's work, little different to the thousands that had preceded it and much the same as the thousands that, God willing, lay ahead. He had taken his flock out that morning and had spent the day watching them eat and move, move and eat. He had decided to drive them back to the homestead camp a little earlier than usual; it was a Sunday, after all, and Mr. Wills knew that Ned Kenny was not someone to shirk his responsibilities as a shepherd.

As he was leading the flock back to camp, Ned met a lone Aboriginal, an older man they called Paddy, who was from one of the neighbouring tribes. Using a combination of words and gestures, Paddy told the old shepherd that all the white people at the homestead had been killed and that the camp itself had been plundered. Not really believing the Aboriginal, Kenny continued with the flock towards the camp. When close, he walked across to a vantage point, a slightly elevated piece of land that he knew would give him a clear view over the camp. What he saw there made him physically ill.

*   *   *

Another shepherd named Patrick Mahoney lived because he had taken his flock of sheep some distance away from the area where Horace Wills had wanted them pastured. The Aboriginals sent out to kill him had returned to the homestead when they couldn't find him. Mahoney saw a fire springing up at the homestead camp and, although well over a kilometre from there, he could clearly hear yells and screams coming from the camp. Guessing what was happening, Mahoney fled into some nearby scrub and hid there for the next 24 hours.

*   *   *

John Moore called out to Ned Kenny and walked from his hiding place to join his fellow shepherd. Knowing what they would find, and horrified by that knowledge, the two men determined to enter the homestead camp to see if there was anyone, or anything, that they could save or salvage; there wasn't. The only living thing in the immediate vicinity was Horace's horse, Simon, saddled and ready to go, and tethered to a dray not 20 metres from where his owner lay dead on the ground.

In one sudden movement, Moore untied the horse and leapt into the saddle. He told Kenny that he was going to Rainworth Station to seek assistance and ignored Kenny's plea to be allowed to ride behind him.

With a final call to Kenny to find refuge in a safe place and a guarantee that he would return with others, Moore wheeled the horse and rode away. Kenny watched him until he disappeared. Conscious now of the unnatural silence of the campsite, Ned Kenny looked around one last time and then set off in the direction Moore had taken. It would probably take him most of a day but he, too, was going to Rainworth Station.

*   *   *

John Moore rode up to the Rainworth Station homestead at around 1.00 a.m. the following morning. He quickly roused James Gregson and told him the story of the Aboriginal' attack on Cullinlaringo. Moore said he believed the only survivors of the attack were another shepherd and himself. Gregson was all action; he woke his stockmen and began to issue orders and directions. Some of the men were sent to neighbouring stations to pass on the news of the attack, and to ask for volunteers to join Gregson in order to visit Cullinlaringo and then, possibly, seek the perpetrators of the outrage. He also wrote a brief note outlining what had happened and sent one of his men to carry the note to the headquarters of the Native Police outside Rockhampton.

By late afternoon, the messengers Gregson had sent out had returned, most accompanied by two or three other men, settlers and their stockmen. At sunset, Gregson led the combined party out towards Cullinlaringo; it comprised several station owners, their men and two native trackers who had worked for Gregson before. The party reached Wills homestead campsite around midnight and set up their own small camp nearby. They would wait for daylight to examine the scene.

In the morning, Gregson's party found 13 bodies scattered around the main campsite, ten of them in and around the inner circle of tents. It appeared that some of the killers had entered the women's and children's tents from the rear. It also appeared that none of the adults had an opportunity to call out a warning to the others. They found Horace Wills' body about two metres from the front door of his tent. They surmised that he had run from his tent when he heard the unmistakable sound of people fighting for their lives. Horace was lying on his back, and there was a shotgun near his outstretched left hand. In his right hand was the revolver he had taken from his son; one shot had been fired from it.

They supposed that Horace had taken just a couple of steps from his tent when he was forced to fire his pistol. He did not have a chance to fire again and was most probably felled by a blow to the head delivered by at least one war club. There was evidence of several further blows to the head from such clubs. Horace's body had several other wounds; there was a deep gash on his right cheek, delivered by a tomahawk or axe, while his head had been almost severed from his body by a single axe stroke. Gregson believed that Horace was already dead when those blows were delivered.

The tent closest to Horace's was a large one occupied by Patrick Manion, his wife and their several children. There were several bodies scattered on the ground around it. A few metres from Horace's body and close to the wall of the Manion tent lay the body of 10-year-old Margaret Manion, killed by several blows to the head. She appeared to have been sitting in the shade of the tent, nursing her little sister and reading a prayer book when she was killed. The little sister was just six months old, and Mrs. Manion seemed to have been trying to protect her daughters when she was also struck down. They were all killed by war clubs and their bodies were found close to Margaret's.

Nearby was the tent occupied by Tom Baker and his family. Mrs. Baker was found dead and partly undressed near the side of the tent. She had been killed by repeated blows to the head. In one hand was some material she had been sewing when she was killed. The Baker's 20-year-old daughter, also partly undressed, was found with her skull crushed, lying in the doorway of the tent. Gregson did not believe that either woman had been interfered with but surmised that they had both taken some of their outer garments off because of the heat inside their tent. In the doorway of that tent, on the inside, lay the bodies of two more of the Baker children. The seven-month-old baby girl and five-year-old had both been killed by blows to the head.

On the other side of the homestead paddock, they found the body of James Scott, the party's cook. Unlike the others, Scott had been up and about, and his body was close to his cooking fire and camp oven. He had been brought down by a spear, which remained embedded in his abdomen, then finished off by blows to the head.

About 50 metres away, near a brush fence he had been working on, they found the body of Patrick Manion. Manion seemed to have put up quite a fight for his life, and his shirt and upper garments had been torn off as he struggled desperately against overwhelming numbers. He had eventually been killed by a number of blows to the head, inflicted by clubs and an axe. Not far away, inside the holding pen that Manion had been working on, they found the body of one of the farm labourers, killed in the same manner of the others but wearing nothing but a flannel shirt.

A few metres beyond the holding pen, they found the bodies of George Elliott — a bullock driver — and one of the station hands. Both had been killed by repeated blows to the head. Elliott still had his stockwhip firmly gripped in his hand. The men had just completed putting a team of oxen into their yokes and attaching them to a dray. During the attack, those oxen had panicked; three had strangled themselves in their own harnesses.

Gregson despatched a small party to see if they could find either survivors or, he thought more likely, the bodies of the rest of the party. Down the creek, about two kilometres from the homestead camp, they found the bodies of the overseer, Tom Baker, his son David and one of the party's shepherds. It appeared that the three men had been establishing a shepherd's camp there for a large flock of ewes and lambs that were grazing peacefully nearby. It also appeared that the men were in the process of putting up a tent when they were attacked, and that they had fought back.

Using tent poles to keep their attackers at bay, the three men had been gradually forced back to the base of a large tree and made a final stand there. Their bodies were found at the foot of the tree, and from the number of gashes and indentations on the tree behind them, it appeared that they died there under a literal shower of war clubs thrown from close range. All three died from repeated blows to the head, while the leg of one of the men had been almost severed by a post-mortem blow from a woodsman's axe.

As they scoured the area, Gregson's men found the body of Tom Baker's dog, its skull crushed. About a kilometre out onto the stony plain they found the body of another of the older shepherds, Henry Watt. Satisfied that there was nothing else to find in that direction, the men wrapped the bodies in canvas and returned with them to the homestead camp.

*   *   *

James Gregson made the decision to bury the bodies as soon as possible and directed some of the men to dig two graves, one of normal dimensions and the other a much larger, mass grave. Horace was laid to rest in the single grave, and all the others placed carefully in the mass grave. All were lowered into the ground with some reverence, the two mothers with their children, the others lying straight and dignified. Gregson read the funeral service over both graves, and then instructed that they be filled in.

Afterwards, the men divided into two working parties. Some men were sent off to collect and return with the various flocks of sheep, which by then had scattered far and wide. The second group then collected as much of the material that had been scattered around the campsite as they could, placing it in caches. The tents were almost completely empty of contents. Boxes and cases had been dragged outside and broken open, and books, paper, crockery, cutlery and other utensils removed. Objects with no obvious utility were simply cast aside. Strangely, the large supplies of sugar, tea, tobacco and flour appeared to have been left largely untouched.

Late in the afternoon, Tom Wills rode into Cullinlaringo. He had learned of the attack the previous evening and had ridden hard throughout the day; he was distraught when he learned the circumstances of his father's death, perhaps blaming himself for not being more forceful in expressing his premonition of possible trouble to his father. Around the same time as Tom Wills rode into camp, Gregson's outriders discovered two more bodies out on the plain, a kilometre or so from the camp. They were the bodies of George Ling, an original member of the overlanding party, and Old Tom, a shepherd they had hired from Rockhampton. On Gregson's orders, the men were buried where their bodies had been found. It brought the total number killed in the attack to 19.

*   *   *

The scattered stock were rounded up and brought back to the holding pens at the homestead paddock. While some men were doing that, others were securing everything that remained at Cullinlaringo and loading the bundles they had made onto the remaining drays. Both tasks were completed by 22 October, and by then Gregson's original rescue party had been supplemented by several other armed settlers. Gregson divided this larger group in two. One party would remain with Tom Wills at Cullinlaringo to help him collect and protect the stock. If necessary, they could take that stock and the rest of the material to Rainworth Station. The second group, comprising 11 men, was going after the killers.

The previous afternoon, Gregson had despatched a small scouting party to identify which direction the marauders had taken. Some eight kilometres to the west of the homestead camp, they found the site where the Aboriginals had camped overnight after fleeing Wills' camp. Alongside the trail they followed to that campsite, they found the remains of several sheep the Aboriginals had killed for food, and there were a lot of abandoned items around the now-deserted campsite. The scouting party then returned to Cullinlaringo to tell Gregson what they had found.

Gregson's pursuit party found the tracks of the fleeing Aboriginals very easy to follow over all but the stoniest ground. At the Nogoa River, they found a cache of material left behind with the probable intention of it being recovered at a later date. The material was hidden beneath bark which had been stripped from nearby trees for that purpose. On the second evening of the pursuit, around two hours before sundown, they located the Aboriginal' camp in thick brigalow scrub, part of the Snake Range, about 35 kilometres from the site of the killings at Cullinlaringo.

The men carefully took up positions overlooking the camp during the night, and at dawn Gregson sent one man back to bring their horses closer as the other ten moved forward into firing positions. They had previously agreed they would all hold their fire until Gregson shot first. The Aboriginal' camp had started to stir as the sun rose on a new day — it was now Wednesday — with a number of campfires being rekindled, and one man amusing others by pretending to read a newspaper. It was this man Gregson selected as his target, and his initial shot was followed by several volleys fired in quick succession.

Those in the camp — which the Europeans estimated to be holding around 200 people — scattered as soon as they realised they were under attack. In the shooting, which was brief but furious, around 30 Aboriginals were killed or wounded, with most of those wounded being helped from the scene by others. After the Aboriginals had fled, Gregson and his men came down to inspect the campsite. Among items taken from the Wills party they recovered there were two watches, some papers, books, powder and knives. Gregson's men collected over 200 spears, a similar number of boomerangs and many other wooden tools and implements; all were burned in a large bonfire.

Conscious that the scrubby nature of the surrounding countryside would be an impediment to any further pursuit of the fleeing Aboriginal, Gregson's party returned to Cullinlaringo and from there to their own stations. Gregson would write a report about what had happened and forward it to the Native Police; all were confident that they would finish the job that Gregson's men had started. As luck would have it, as he approached Rainworth, Gregson came across a party of Native Police, headed by Lieutenant Cave, who were on their way to the headwaters of the Nogoa River to do just that.

*   *   *

A terrible retribution followed. Two days after the Gregson attack, a party of Native Police, probably the one under Lieutenant Cave's command, found another Aboriginal camp further to the west. Firearms from Cullinlaringo were spotted there, and that was enough to condemn the camp's inhabitants. Another dawn attack resulted in a death toll estimated to be upwards of 50. In the months following Cullinlaringo, up to 300 Aboriginal men, women and children were shot down to punish Aboriginals in general, and to teach them a lesson. It seems to have been more a European venting of rage than any sort of planned legal or social response to the fate of the Wills party. It was also something which

Horace himself would have condemned because, above all else, he would have seen that nothing positive could come of it. No matter how many mountains he, figuratively and literally, had to cross, Horace always did so because he believed the future should always be better than the past. Everyone's future, that is.

ALL THEIR TOMORROWS

Sometime much, much later — months certainly, and years possibly — one of the survivors of the tribe whose members had attacked the Wills party (and who themselves were almost completely destroyed afterwards) told the story of the killings from the Aboriginal side. This unknown survivor told the Europeans then living at Cullinlaringo, some Wills among them, that there had been an ongoing argument in the tribe about how to treat with Horace and the others after they arrived and began to set up their operations beyond Separation Creek.

The elders of the tribe were adamant, from the time of the Wills party's arrival, that all members of the party must be killed to avenge the deaths of the two young men shot down by the Native Police earlier. Horace's open and sincere policy of peaceful coexistence caused some members of the tribe to question the plans to kill them all, and after two weeks of Horace's policy, some of the younger members of the tribe began to ask openly why the white people needed to be killed. In a possible effort to head off what may have become a direct questioning of their authority, the elders ordered an immediate attack.

Around 2 p.m. on the designated day, the tribe's warriors made their way into Wills camp, individually and in twos and threes. They did not carry their weapons openly, fearing that this would tip off their plans to the Europeans, instead hiding them behind their bodies and tucked into their belts. The warriors then carefully placed themselves near their intended victims and, at a given signal, simultaneously attacked those victims. As his body indicated, Horace had burst from his tent, shotgun in one hand and revolver in the other. He was able to fire a single shot at the first warrior who rushed him, the bullet grazing the inside of that man's right arm but was simultaneously grabbed by two other warriors and struck down by a third.

*   *   *

It took Elizabeth Wills a month or more to accept the reality of what had happened to her partner of almost 30 years. When she finally did, Elizabeth wrote to Cedric, Horace and Egbert at their school in Germany. She told her sons of their father's death, and how in excess of 350 Aboriginals had been killed in the aftermath, noting simply that the Sydney newspapers said that the innocent should not have been made to suffer along with the guilty.

The baby Elizabeth bore just before the death of her husband was a little girl she named Hortense Sarah Spencer Wills, with Hortense chosen as it was the closest female name to Horace. Elizabeth, her baby and the other small children remained at Belle Vue after Horace's death. In 1876, the property was sold and Elizabeth moved to Melbourne where she stayed with her relatives, the Colden Antill Harrison's. Elizabeth Wills was described as "Australia's oldest colonist" when she died, aged 90, at her daughter's home in Newtown, Geelong, in December 1907. She left seven children, 36 grandchildren and 17 great grandchildren.

Most of those who remembered Elizabeth in her later years would recall her as being sharp with people, quick to find fault and seeming to view the world through jaundiced eyes. Had they known her before Horace's death, they would have known a very different woman. When

Horace and Elizabeth arrived at Ararat in 1840, they were on the brink of establishing one of Australia's greatest pastoral runs. Not only would new products and techniques be discovered and introduced there, a large family of active children would be raised and educated in one of the district's finest homes. When Ararat, the township they had helped to found was to be incorporated, the town elders searched around for a motto and eventually selected, "I bring joy". They did so on the recollections of Horatio and Elizabeth Wills on what coming to, and living in, the district had brought to them individually and to the family who called the area home.

*   *   *

Tom Wills was broken in some way by the death of his father and would live most of the rest of his life flirting with demons that only he could see. One week after the killings, Tom wrote a long letter to the Colonial Secretary in Brisbane, asking that a troop of Native Police be stationed at Cullinlaringo. He had remained at the station with the other survivors and several hired or loaned farm labourers in an attempt to establish a viable farming enterprise there. He was still at Cullinlaringo when he again wrote to the Colonial Secretary in January 1862, reiterating his earlier call for police protection. In this second letter, Tom also pointed out that the entire frontier in that region was open to further depredations and that he believed that one of his neighbours was sheltering some of his father's killers.

Cedric Wills returned to Belle Vue from Germany in July 1862 and was despatched north almost immediately to help Tom at Cullinlaringo, where problems were emerging. Tom had developed the habit of leaving the property for weeks at a time, travelling back to Melbourne to play in inter-colonial and other cricket matches with his friends. Because of this, the trustees of Horace's estate would dismiss Tom as manager in 1864. Seeing this dismissal as an opportunity, Tom became a professional cricketer, playing for whoever would support him while also playing Australian Rules in the off-season, helping to grow and develop the game he had pioneered.

In 1864, Tom Wills was instrumental in the formation and preparation of the first Australian cricket team to tour England, a team of Aboriginals from Victoria's Western District, including some from the region where Tom had grown up at Lexington. Tom and the team parted ways before it left Australian shores. Tom never married, although he did have a de facto wife in later years. Alcohol abuse ruined his sporting prowess, and his life. In May 1880, soon after being released from a psychiatric hospital, Thomas Wentworth Wills committed suicide shortly after his 45th birthday.

Emily Wills, probably the first European child to be born in the Ararat area, would become the mainstay of her mother's life after Horace was killed. On 10 November 1864, she married her cousin — and her brother Tom's best friend — Henry Colden Antill Harrison — in the little St. John's Church at Point Henry; the newly-installed plaque to her father's memory looked down upon the service. Harrison, who was another outstanding colonial athlete and who would come to be regarded as the father of Australian football, was also a successful businessman and the Harrisons lived a life of some comfort in Melbourne.

Horace and Egbert Wills followed Cedric home from school in Germany, the boys arriving back at Belle Vue on 18 December 1862. Cedric had succeeded Tom as manager at Cullinlaringo, but fared little better than his older brother, his explosive temper alienating most potential overseers at the property. He remained at Cullinlaringo until 1892, and descendants of all three Wills brothers still farm and live in the district.

The death of Horace Wills and his 18 companions did not receive anywhere near the attention that the quality of their lives demanded. A week after the news of what had occurred at Cullinlaringo reached Melbourne, news of another Wills swamped all reporting. The fate of the Burke and Wills expedition dominated all reporting for weeks to come. In some respects, this has meant that Horace Wills' life has been undervalued and this, I suspect, is very much what he would have wanted. He was a man who lived for the challenges that life offered, and he was more successful than most. All men die; few have the opportunity to die in the midst of the latest grand adventure they have planned.

A NOTE ON SOURCES

Much of the individual stories that make up *The Other Side of the Mountain* come from contemporary reporting, and much of that reporting is from early Australian newspapers. When I first began to collect material for stories like the three contained in this book, those newspapers were viewed in microfiche at the various state libraries or at the National Library of Australia, then and now one of Australia's great cultural institutions. Research is so much easier now, though, through the ongoing expansion of the National Library's "Trove," its digital online newspaper service. It is a resource that is almost literally priceless and one which has contributed to this and many other works.

Ralph Entwistle's brief time in the spotlight of history is well-documented in contemporary newspapers and the letters to the various editors that his exploits generated make fascinating, and sometimes funny, reading. A good background to the events can be found in such works as Charles White's *History of Australian Bushranging* (Lloyd O'Neil, Hawthorn, 1970), Frank Clune's *Wild Colonial Boys* (Angus and Robertson, Sydney, 1982) and John O'Sullivan's *Mounted Police in NSW,* (Rigby, Adelaide, 1979).

The story of John Horrocks and his bête noir, Harry the camel, is drawn primarily from newspaper accounts from the 1840s and later, as various people associated with Horrocks and Penwortham penned their recollections of pioneering days in South Australia. More literary accounts can be found in several booklets and pamphlets put together by

South Australian local history societies. The National Library, and several state libraries have copies of these. Accounts of the life and struggles of Samuel T Gill also contain relevant material, particularly his notes on the Northern Expedition. Copies of these are available at several sites. The National Library also holds press cuttings about Horrocks, Gill and all the other main characters in the stories.

The considerable contribution Horace Wills made to the pastoral industry in three colonies has been shaded by the circumstances of his death and the short, bright sporting career of his oldest son, Thomas Wentworth Wills. Contemporary newspapers in all three colonies cover different aspects of Wills life, while Greg De Moore's *Tom Wills*, (Allen and Unwin, Crow's Nest, 2008) and Les Perrin's *Cullinlaringo*, (self-published, McDowall, 1998) give more literary backgrounds. In 1985, I wrote a piece also called *Cullinlaringo* for the Royal Historical Society of Victoria's journal. It provides a much more concise account of the events described in *The Other Side of the Mountain*.

ALSO AVAILABLE FROM WOODSLANE PRESS

Outback
The discovery of
Australia's interior
By Derek Parker
$24.99
ISBN: 9781921203923

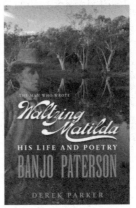

Banjo Paterson
The man who wrote
Waltzing Matilda
By Derek Parker
$29.99
ISBN: 9781921683473

The Only way Home
One woman, two donkeys
and an extraordinary outback
journey of healing and renewal
By Liz Byron
$24.99
ISBN: 9781925868203

Arthur Phillip
Australia's first Governor
By Derek Parker
$29.99
ISBN: 9781921683480

Bligh in Australia
A new appraisal of William Bligh
and the Rum Rebellion
By Russell Earls Davis
$29.99
ISBN: 9781921683503

Governor Macquarie
His life, times and revolutionary
vision for Australia
By Derek Parker
$29.99
ISBN: 9781921606915

WOODSLANE
PRESS

www.woodslane.com.au